LOS ANGELES

AN ILLUSTRATED HISTORY

LOS ANGELES

AN ILLUSTRATED HISTORY

BY BRUCE HENSTELL

ALFRED A. KNOPF · NEW YORK · 1980

Produced for Alfred A. Knopf, Inc. by

 Rosebud Books, Inc.
8777 Lookout Mountain Avenue
Los Angeles, CA 90046

Design by Alex D'Anca

Library of Congress Cataloging in Publication Data

Henstell, Bruce.
  Los Angeles, an illustrated history.

  Includes index.
    1. Los Angeles—History—Pictorial works. 2. Los
Angeles—Description—Views.   I. Title.
F869.L843H46   1980   979.4'94   80-7642
ISBN 0-394-50941-2

To
My Mother and My Father
For Having Been Here.

Contents

List of Illustrations

Photo Credits

Anonymous private collections: 40, 43, 46, 50, 51, 59, 61, 62, 67, 70, 78, 84, 90, 91, 117, 120, 121, 125, 126, 127, 129, 131, 132, 133, 134, 135, 136, 137, 138, 139, 149, 151, 154, 158, 160, 162, 163, 164, 175, 198, 199, 220

Bill Beebe: 144, 146, 169, 176 180, 181

Bancroft Library, University of California, Berkeley: 39, 64, 65, 66, 68, 69, 72, 209

Beverly Hills Public Library: 138, 214.

California Historical Society, Los Angeles: 3, 6, 10, 20, 24, 25, 26, 27, 28, 32, 33, 34, 35, 37, 39, 43, 44, 45, 47, 48, 49, 50, 51, 52, 53, 54, 58, 59, 60, 61, 63, 68, 70, 74, 76, 77, 78, 79, 80, 81, 83, 84, 85, 88, 89, 92, 93, 95, 117, 118, 119, 124, 128, 130, 131, 137, 145, 152, 154, 165, 170, 171, 189, 192, 199, 200, 206, 218, 221

Collection of the Author: 17, 18, 189, 215

A. F. Gilmore Company: 204

Bruce Henstell: 210, 211, 212, 214, 216, 217

Huntington Library: 22, 23, 38, 42, 45, 46, 47, 48, 52, 54, 56, 59, 60, 61, 66, 67, 70, 71, 72, 80, 81, 90, 94, 122, 123, 124, 126, 137, 168, 169, 171, 179, 187, 188, 210

KTLA: 194, 195, 196, 197

Los Angeles County Museum of Natural History: 16, 28, 29, 33, 37, 125, 129, 219

Los Angeles Department of Water and Power: 82

Los Angeles Dodgers, Inc.: 205, 222

Los Angeles Police Department: 149

Los Angeles Public Library: 26, 30, 53, 143, 164, 165

Pasadena Public Library: 44

Pasadena Tournament of Roses Association: 150, 202, 203

Santa Monica Public Library: 48, 64

Southern California Rapid Transit District: 9, 91, 122, 180, 187

Southern Pacific Company: 36, 38, 47, 72, 155

Sunkist: 62, 63

University of California, Los Angeles, Department of Special Collections: 37, 53, 55, 69, 79, 82, 83, 94, 95, 114, 121, 124, 127, 129, 131, 133, 134, 145, 146, 147, 148, 149, 154, 155, 156, 157, 159, 163, 170, 171, 172, 173, 174, 177, 178, 179, 181, 182, 183, 186, 188, 190, 191, 192, 193, 197, 198, 204, 219, 220

Thomas P. Vinetz: 208, 209, 212, 213, 214, 216

Whittington Collection, Huntington Library: 116, 118, 119, 126, 135, 140, 142, 143, 144, 147, 152, 153, 158, 160, 161, 162, 166, 172, 179, 180, 183, 184, 186, 194, 211, 213

Welton Becket Associates: 200, 201, 215

COLOR SECTION

Anonymous private collection: 106–107

Collection of the Author: 109

Environmental Communications: 109

Bryan Gindoff Collections (postcard art): 98, 99, 101, 103

Huntington Library: 99, 108

Los Angeles County Museum of Natural History: 97, 100, 101, 102, 104–105

Pasadena Tournament of Roses Association: 98

Diana Peterson: 112

Thomas P. Vinetz: 103, 110, 111

The Los Angeles photo gallery of Pierce and Blanchard, ca. 1890. Blanchard, with pince-nez and elegant goatee, sits on the left; Mrs. Blanchard on the right. C.C. Pierce is behind the camera. Pierce was a commercial photographer in Los Angeles for fifty years, from the 1890s to the 1940s, and an inveterate collector of photographs as well. In time, his singular holdings came to constitute one of the major photographic resources for the history of the city. Today his collection is maintained by the California Historical Society at Los Angeles.

Acknowledgments

Many have contributed to the present work, have given of their energy, time, good will and most importantly, of their good cheer. I am deeply grateful.

First and foremost to the librarians, curators and archivists, indispensable partners in a project such as this. I've been fortunate to encounter those whose respect for the materials under their care is matched by their kindness. My special thanks to the staff of the Department of Special Collections, University Research Library, University of California at Los Angeles, whose congeniality has made the library a second home: to James Mink, head of the Department and University Archivist; Hilda Bohem, public services librarian and curator for pictorial materials, a constant source of wise advice; Pearl Rosenfelt and Dan Luckenbill who have coped with a series of outrageous demands.

To the Huntington Library, and Alan Jutzi, associate curator of rare books, a model of generosity and assistance.

To the Los Angeles County Museum of Natural History, and Bill Mason, curator, and John Cahoon, curatorial assistant.

And to the staffs of a number of other institutions and collections: the California Historical Society, Los Angeles History Center, and director Carolyn Ditte Wagner; the Pasadena Tournament of Roses Association, and Frosty Foster, Susan Hawksworth and Ed Pierce; the A.F. Gilmore Company, and Hank Hilty; the Southern California Rapid Transit District, and Nola Wolf; Wells Fargo Bank History Room, and Elaine Guilleran and Joan W. Salz; the California Historical Society, San Francisco; the Southern Pacific Company, and William Robertson; the Sunkist Company, and Deborah Lindine; Weldon Beckett Associates, and Stuart Oreck and Donna Joffrion; Environmental Communications, and David Greenberg; Bill Beebe; Foster and Kleiser, and Joseph Blackstock; the Pasadena Public Library, and Joyce Penny; the Los Angeles Dodgers; television station KTLA, and Mary Barrow; the Los Angeles Police Department, and Lt. Dan Cooke; the History Room of the Los Angeles Public Library; the Beverly Hills Public Library, and a number of others who, for various reasons, are not listed here. To all, and to any I have inadvertently omitted: thank you.

Without Don Ackland and the staff of Rosebud Books, this project would never have come to pass. Once again the editorial skills of Anita Keys and her *sang-froid* have proved indispensable. Bryan Gindoff has given of his support. Ed Mosk and Robert Getz have aided this book in a manner I cannot fully thank them for. I would as well acknowledge the many contributions of: Doug and Ruth Holis, Femmy DeLyser, Naomi Berger Davidson, Harriet Katz, Richard and Wendy Kahlenberg, Doug Ring and, last but especially, my friends at *Los Angeles Magazine* whose many favors great and small I greatly appreciate; to Geoff Miller, editor, Judith Grout, and the rest of the staff.

There is another fact that unites the names above other than their contributions. And that is, all are proud of the city of Los Angeles.

Los Angeles became a nerve center and entrepôt of war and, in war, the interurbans, the Los Angeles Railway, held a special responsibility. And a special need for manpower which was soon being partially met by the rapid recruitment of motormanettes and conductorettes. In June of 1944, the system's most noticeable and desperate advertisement for more enlistees appeared on Los Angeles streets, the so-called "Flying Tiger" car.

Preface

Los Angeles: An Illustrated History is an attempt to get all the people who have ever made up the city of Los Angeles to sit still long enough for a group portrait. It has not been easy and at first might be thought more than slightly chimerical in nature.

The problems have been more than just finding a mutually convenient day for a sitting. Los Angeles was founded in 1781, alas photography was not invented until the early part of the nineteenth century. Even after invention, photography was an unwieldy technology and by the time it had been simplified enough to travel from its points of origin in Europe west to America and thence further west to Southern California, a good deal of Los Angeles life had passed from the current into the realm of history.

It is not certain which is absolutely the earliest photographic image of Los Angeles. The first date from the early 1860s in spite of a well-known and much-reproduced image of the Los Angeles plaza which repeatedly has been called the earliest photograph and dated to the 1850s (it appears on page 34). Unfortunately, it shows a structure which was not built until the early 1860s and therefore certainly has been mislabeled.

By the 1860s, cameras were here and photographers were using them to record the life of the frontier city of Los Angeles. Yet a further technological problem clouds our appreciation of the life of those days. The photographs of the 1860s, 1870s and even into the 1890s are mostly of serene cityscapes and landscapes, showing motionless or

The beach and Lick Pier at Ocean Park, ca. the late 1920s. Sandwiched between Santa Monica to the north and Venice to the south, Ocean Park had two side-by-side piers and was one of the earliest Los Angeles seaside resorts. Later its municipal sovereignty was absorbed into its two neighboring cities. Its piers fell into disrepair and were eventually removed in the mid-1970s.

at least very slowly moving things and people. Inanimate objects, empty or nearly empty streets (the few people visible, as often as not, stare hypnotically into the camera), studio portraits of residents in their Sunday best, abound. Of city life—teeming streets, busy markets, blacksmith stalls, courtrooms, jails, offices—we have little. The reason was, simply, that neither the cameras nor the photographic films of the day were sufficiently fast to capture life as it passed. Things had to be made to stop or at least slow down for the camera. Streets were photographed when people weren't around to cause blurrs. A charming example of this is the photograph of the family Lugo on page 29 where the adults stand rock-like but the baby couldn't be coaxed to remain still.

That early photography worked to eliminate people from their cities is a special handicap for this book. Photographs of streets and buildings are interesting and important, especially in documenting physical growth, and Los Angeles, among the world's cities, has had spectacular physical growth. But the essence of this city is, as Louis Mumford has pointed out, as a container for people's activities. And it is the detail of these activities that this book has tried to capture for Los Angeles.

Once cameras acquired rapid shutters, once films were fast enough to free the photographer from the maddening task of trying to get his subjects, and any interlopers in the background, to stand perfectly still, the record of the life of Los Angeles becomes considerably richer. Still, large parts, whole sections of our projected group portrait will be found to be missing.

In relative terms, photographs cost considerably more then than they do now. So they were taken by the rich or by those whose purpose was to capture images people elsewhere might order or tourists might buy as souvenirs. So a great many of our palm trees are preserved for immortality, but much of Los Angeles' social life and, most important, its ethnic groups, are not.

Photographs were ordered by families to record certain high-points in the rhythm of life. Ironically, sadly, many of these have not survived. They were put away, forgotten, inadvertently destroyed, left behind. Moreover, families tend to feel somebody will always be around who knows exactly who the faded face in the photograph is and what the circumstances were which dictated the making of the image, as in the photograph of (as inscribed on the back of the original) "Uncle Erreld in his Maori costume." It will be difficult, I suspect, to ever place Uncle Erreld in his proper place in our great Los Angeles group portrait.

Even when a photograph carries specific information, it can't always be trusted. Lynchings were once a frequent occurrence in Los Angeles yet few photographs survive

(Left)
The Lugo home faced the Plaza and was in turn a residence, a hospital, a college and a Chinese restaurant.

(Opposite Top)
A credible enough lynching; somewhere but not Los Angeles. The trees are the giveaway: definitely un-Southern Californian. The entrances to corrals, with their conveniently high cross members, were the locally preferred dispatch areas.

(Opposite Left)
In this decidedly simulated street scene, a group of doctors and their automobiles strike a pose in front of the California Hospital.

(Opposite Right)
Uncle Erreld was dressed up and, one hopes, he had somewhere to go. And that he didn't get arrested getting there.

to show us this fact of early life. One, in a major collection, clearly shows a lynching and has been identified as Los Angeles by some who should know better. It is in fact an errant motion picture still. Another, reproduced here, is a real lynching but evidence, chiefly the trees, make it highly unlikely as Los Angeles. Or, a favorite of mine, a real photograph of the famous 1910 Dominguez Hills air meet, shows a cavalcade of majestic airships cruising past the packed grandstand. Each of these devices did fly at Dominguez. Unfortunately not all at once. The photograph is a composite, a trick of the laboratory.

So photographs aren't always what they say they are. Neither are all the details of past life preserved in photographs: consider how much has missed the camera's eye! We are confronting a jigsaw puzzle then, one which comes boxed with no picture of what when assembled it is to be. History from documents and records provides an outline. The colors, the texture of life as lived in Los Angeles is missing. What follows is an attempt to supply that life, suggest the colors.

Old photographs are not just antiques, nor just quaint reminders. These pieces of information are the foundation upon which the future, whether we realize it or not, has already been placed. To ignore this information is to risk diminishing or losing altogether the diversity and vibrancy of the Los Angeles to come.

Maps

The Indians first owned California but the Spanish shoved them aside. In the name of the king, vast tracts of land were awarded first to the missions and next to the pueblos as they were formed (Los Angeles in 1781). To hold the province, an army of occupation—although that overstates the reality to moderns—was stationed. It was quiet duty and there was time for pleasant thoughts such as raising cattle, provided there was land upon which to do it. And, as soldiers have reasoned from time immemorial, it was not too much to ask that conquered territory be shared with loyal servants. In 1784, the first title was given out. Juan Dominguez was sixty-four and a veteran of the original Portolá expedition. He settled in an area a few hours' hard ride south of Los Angeles. The 43,000 acres he requested and received title to he called Rancho San Pedro. Corporal Juan Verdugo got 36,000 acres from near Mission San Gabriel to where the Arroyo Seco encountered the Los Angeles River. In other words, a good slice of East Los Angeles. So it went until the entire basin had been spoken for. The last grant went, ironically perhaps, to an American, Thomas Robbins, and it was the island of Santa Catalina.

The borders of these grants were ill-defined and frequently relied on features of the land which, in time, lived only in the memory of the oldest settlers. The Californios hardly cared; but the Americans with their strict legalities and their housing tracts and their cities cared very much about precise definition. A lands' commission was appointed by the federal government to pass upon Spanish claims and, in the difficult process of defending themselves against trespassers and interlopers, the descendents of the original grantees lost their titles and passed, for the most part, from the scene.

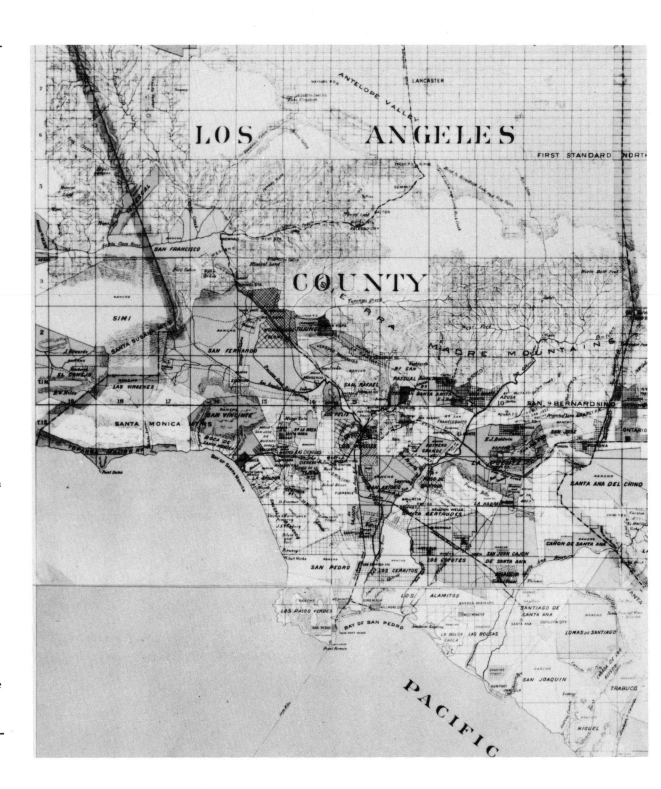

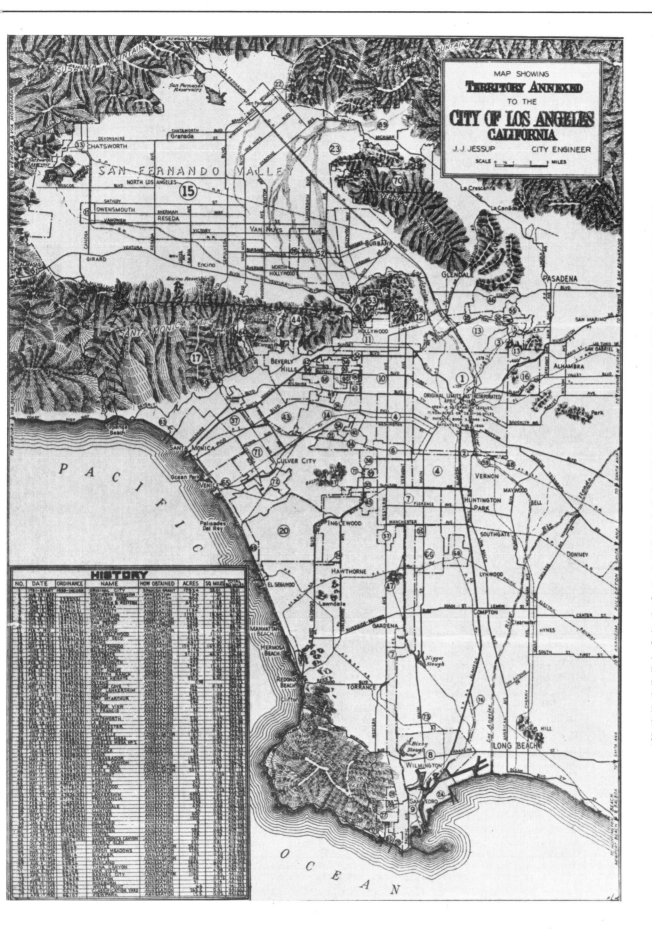

At its beginning, under the Spanish Laws of the Indies, Los Angeles was granted for a municipal patrimony four square leagues of land, a league being equal to about two and three-fifths miles. At first, Los Angeles lived off its capital, selling land to whoever it could con into buying it for whatever it could get. The proceeds kept the city government afloat though sometimes just barely, since many sales passed without the appearance of a purchaser. In the 1890s, city fathers realized a paradox. They could acquire almost endless amounts of new city land and make money from same without the bother of having to sell. All the city had to do was expand its jurisdiction and then tax the land it had acquired.

There were other factors operating in the constant expansion of the city of Los Angeles. One was municipal pride. Early on, there was a question as to whether Los Angeles or Pasadena would dominate the basin and Los Angeles businessmen were intent on making it their city. Then there was the harbor. Los Angeles was nowhere near the water but when a harbor was built at the turn of the century, the city decided it had fought the battle to get the funds and deserved the prize of administering the new property. So the "shoestring" was laid out. A continuous band of territory, as specified under the state constitution, stretched south, barely a block wide at some points, until it hit water and then expanded as much as neighboring cities would allow.

The next round of annexations came with the building of the Los Angeles Aqueduct in the early twentieth century. Drink our water, said Los Angeles, share our bill. Which meant a surrender of municipal sovereignty by smaller entities and a comingling with the giant. It was an offer cities with no readily available water could ill afford to refuse. Thereafter, the habit of just growing got into Los Angeles' bones.

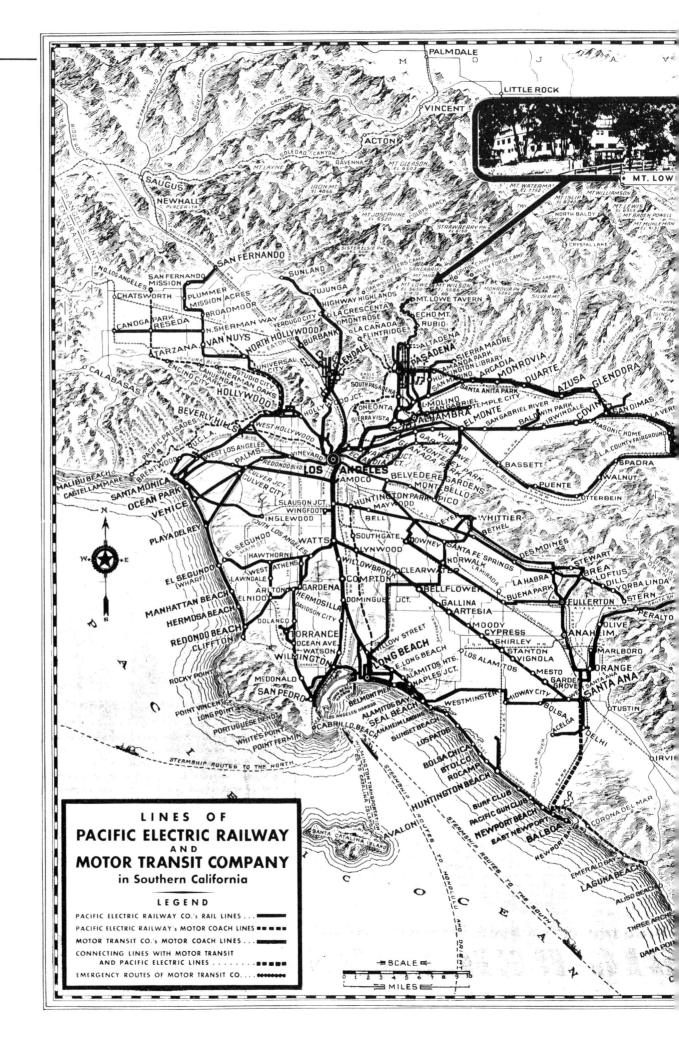

LINES OF
PACIFIC ELECTRIC RAILWAY
AND
MOTOR TRANSIT COMPANY
in Southern California

—

LEGEND

PACIFIC ELECTRIC RAILWAY CO.'s RAIL LINES . . .
PACIFIC ELECTRIC RAILWAY's MOTOR COACH LINES
MOTOR TRANSIT CO.'s MOTOR COACH LINES . . .
CONNECTING LINES WITH MOTOR TRANSIT
AND PACIFIC ELECTRIC LINES . . . .
EMERGENCY ROUTES OF MOTOR TRANSIT CO. . . .

SCALE

0 1 2 3 4 5 6 7 8 9 10
MILES

COPYRIGHT, 1933 BY D.W. PONTIUS FOR PACIFIC ELECTRIC RAILWAY

~DRAWN BY~ GERALD A. EDDY, 1935

The Pacific Electric system, the "big red cars," went most everywhere in Southern California in what the company advertised was "comfort–speed–safety." In the mid-1930s, there were more than 1,000 miles in the system, more than the transit systems of the next five major cities combined. Fifty-six cities were served and almost 66,000,000 total passengers were carried (in 1934). The routes ran from the Olympian heights of Mt. Lowe on whose crest stood the Alpine Tavern and a resort, to the blue Pacific. Mt. Lowe was only $1.50 from Los Angeles and the sea about $1. Despite its coverage, the system was ailing. The glory days for the PE had been when it ran from one widely separated locality to another, along rights of way free from the impertinences of people and automobiles. As the spaces filled in, that advantage was lost. The speed was reduced and the safety? Streetcar–pedestrian and streetcar–automobile crashes were increasingly common.

A vicious cycle was evident: as ridership fell, fares rose to make up the difference with the result that ridership declined even further. Despite boom days in World War II, the handwriting was on the wall. As the system sputtered, the taste of government, industry and public for highways grew and so the trolleys were kicked off their tracks and their rights of way acquired for freeways. By the early 1960s, the last "big red car" had completed its last run.

I

A Fair
and
Glorious Land

In 1510 in Spain, there appeared a novel, a work of romantic fantasy entitled "Las Sergas de Esplandian," or, translated, "The Adventures of Esplandian." An undistinguished representative of a perishable genre, this work and its author, Garcia de Montalvo, might have forever remained historical nonentities were it not for one single word. In the novel's plot, Montalvo referred to a fantastic island inhabited by Amazons of incalculable wealth and he called that island "California." This seems to have been the earliest appearance of the word "California" in print: it may have even originated with Montalvo. Unaware as he was of its eventual significance, he left us no memoir of the word's invention.

How exactly Montalvo's word came to be applied to the coast of North America is obscure. One theory is that it was conveyed by Spanish explorers who, in the early sixteenth century, commenced a two-hundred-year-long series of voyages of discovery to the New World. Perhaps the word had been included in the baggage of Hernando Cortés, the conqueror of Mexico who visited Baja, the lower California peninsula. Yet neither Cortés nor Juan Cabrillo, who landed at what is now San Diego in 1542, nor Sebastián Vizcaíno who explored extensively in the early seventeenth century, were exactly the sort to have indulged in the Montalvo brand of romantic fantasy. Certainly neither were their men, the majority of whom probably had trouble reading at all.

By the middle of the eighteenth century, land expeditions were being sent north from Mexico to map and col-

Father Zephpyrin Engelhardt (1851–1934), historian of the California missions, in the mid-1920s. He is inspecting a copy of the original register of Mission San Juan Capistrano, the entries of which are in the hand of his illustrious predecessor and founder of the missions, Father Junipero Serra.

onize California. If once there had been some dim hope the land might prove to ooze gold, it was soon obvious it did not. The goal was rather possession of the territory, especially of its excellent harbors. In 1769, one expedition, headed by Gaspar de Portolá and missionary Father Junipero Serra reached San Diego. In August, a smaller contingent continued north and, according to expedition diarist Father Juan Crespi, after a few days, entered a "spacious valley," making camp by the side of a river. Gabrielino Indians, of Shoshone background, obviously friendly and equally obviously well-to-do, appeared before the transcient Spanish. "Their chief," Crespi notes, "brought some strings of beads made of shells, and they threw us three handfuls of them." Tobacco was smoked. The next morning, the Spanish moved on, unaware that they had just had the honor of becoming the first of their race to spend a night in what is now downtown Los Angeles.

The City

In 1781, to secure California for Spain, a series of pueblos or towns were created, of which the second was Los Angeles. Settlers were recruited by the government through Alta California governor Felipe De Neve, brought to Los Angeles and there, amidst great fanfare it was assumed, founded the city. More likely is that having completed a long, forced march from somewhere in Northern Mexico, the first Angelenos set about, without formality, to the building of shelters and the planting of crops. In 1836, Los Angeles was elevated to the status of a cuidad, or city. The change was cosmetic. The city was still a small oasis in a remote hinterland. It had a reputation for the beauty of its setting, but also for the thieves, gamblers and drifters who inhabited it along with its older, more respectable citizens.

The Missions

The backbone of Spanish California was not the towns but the missions, established in a line north from San Diego under the direction of Father Serra. The missions were to guide the heathens: teach them honest labor and European morality. Later, the Americans scrapped most of the Spanish tradition and influence but created the romantic image of pastoral missions under benign priests. In truth, the guidance of mission fathers could be harsh and even brutal. In 1824, the missions were secularized by the new Republic of Mexico and their properties ordered distributed to the Indians whose labor had created them. However, this did not occur. Instead, the Indians were merely turned loose. The net effect of mission life was that native Indian culture was exterminated and, along with it, the native Indians.

The Californios

The descendents of the first settlers, those who joined them having been irresistibly drawn to faraway places, bureaucrats and military men posted to the pueblo who were paid with land, in time married and had families, elaborating a social order. In the time-honored manner of all frontier people, they soon created a definition of themselves for themselves which set them off from stay-at-homes. They considered themselves cultured, well disposed to guests and visitors, preoccupied not with their immense ranchos or their cattle trade or with mere earthly gain but with the stylish and pleasant passage of life. In this, to all accounts, they were admirably successful.

The Californios demonstrated their gentle mettle in their encounters with a people tempermentally quite different: the Americans. In the early nineteenth century, these newcomers began arriving. Rather than segregating or excluding them, the Californios invited them into their homes and, indeed, their families. Pliny Fiske Temple, a Boston merchant, succeeded (as Don Juan Temple) as did Don Abel Stearns, Don Benito Wilson and a handful of others, all of whom were men of substance with native wives in the dusty pueblo of Los Angeles.

That it was not a thriving city hardly seemed to matter. It had its own pace, given it by its respectables, men conversant with scale. And it had its incredible, its overpowering, natural beauty.

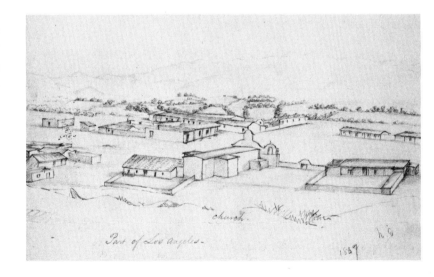

Los Angeles, properly El pueblo de la Reina de los Angeles, was founded on principles set down in the Spanish empire's Laws of the Indies which in turn derived from Roman city planning. A plaza was called for, streets to enter and exit at set, regular angles, oriented towards specific directions. Town lots for the inhabitants and nearby farm plots were detailed. Yet something went wrong. As the town grew, streets developed at strange angles and when, in 1836, the *ayuntamiento,* or city council, appointed a committee to straighten matters out, the effort proved futile.

Fort Moore

American Fort at Pueblo de los Angeles from Mr. Pryor's house — July 10 1847. + Sierra Nevada

Ciudad de los Angeles. March 27th 1848 from the south.

(Above)
In 1847, William Rich Hutton, on a tour of California, stopped in Los Angeles and to him we are indebted for one of our earliest looks at the town. In his sketch of the plaza, the façade of the church, constructed in 1822, can be seen. Of the style of these buildings another visitor wrote: "Few of them . . . have any pretensions to architectural taste, finish, or convenience of plan or arrangement."

The disorder of its buildings mirrored early Los Angeles civic life. The gentile Californios were not the town's sole occupants. The balance of the population, which changed constantly and usually in the middle of the night, was described as "the lowest drunkards and gamblers of the country." Murders were frequent and, when justice was slow, vigilante action was not.

The missions were established under the direction of the ascetic and ubiquitous Franciscan father Junipero Serra. They were meant to hold forth the light of God's word, maintain learning in a community whose elite did not always consider mastery of letters a social advantage, illuminate the land with art, provide hospice for wayfarers and, most of all, convert the native heathens to Western ways and Western religion. The economic structure of the missions depended upon the unrecompensed labor of Indian neophytes, willing or unwilling. The native Indian cultures had been workable, the people serene. The mission fathers insisted on herding the people out of their habitats and onto the mission grounds, there to labor in agricultural pursuits in support of the church. The effects were devastating. Between 1769 and 1834, Franciscan fathers baptized 53,600 adult Indians and buried 37,000. The missions, according to author Carey McWilliams, were no better than "picturesque charnel houses."

In 1834, the Republic of Mexico was declared and the missions were ordered secularized. Their possessions were to be sold, the proceeds distributed among the Indians as a patrimony. Mission fathers protested and delayed. The Indians ended up with nothing and, in the eyes of the community, became objects of pity at best and beasts of burden at worst. By the 1890s, their cultural identity was a thing of the past and as a people they had all but ceased to exist.

In 1771, Mission San Gabriel Archangel was established, the fourth such in Alta California. The first site was along a river, El Rio del Dulcisimo Nombre de Jesus de los Temblores, the River of the Sweet Name of Jesus of the Earthquakes, a

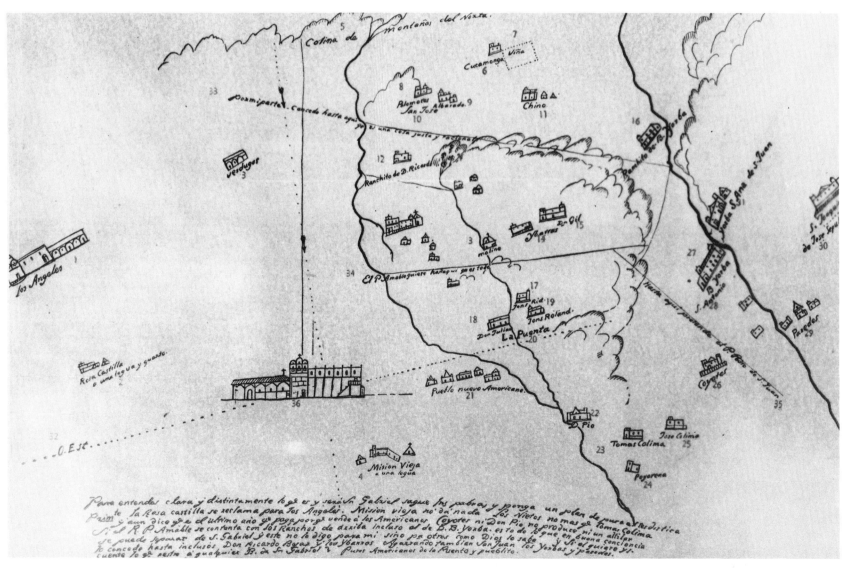

title doubtlessly devised during an earth movement. A few years later, it was realized the river frequently overflowed its banks so the site was moved back.

(Opposite Top)
The Rev. José Godayol, OFM, was received at Santa Barbara in 1854. In 1902 he died, the last Franciscan father in California.

All roads led to Mission San Gabriel. The mission appeared at the center of early settlers and is today about 30 miles from downtown Los Angeles.

(Right)
Mission San Gabriel as it looked in 1885.

A group of unidentified mission fathers, possibly Mission Santa Barbara: the fathers were neither as romantic nor as personable nor even as pacifistic as legend might have it.

(Opposite Top)
A mission Indian woman, ca. 1895.
The few who survived the mission
system were left as historical
curiosities.

A mission Indian man, ca. 1890s.
Those who lived to old age were rare.

Ramona, photographed in northern
Mexico in 1899. At the turn of the
century, Helen Hunt Jackson wrote
Ramona. Her experience paralleled that
of Upton Sinclair a generation later.
Ramona was meant to expose the
brutality of Indian life and the
prejudice the Indians were subjected
to. Stripped of its message of protest,
it made a nice little romance.

(Above)
The cemetery at Mission San Gabriel.

Luis El Cojo, maker of gravemarkers
for Mission San Juan Capistrano,
ca. 1902.

The Californios thought of themselves as *gente de razon*, literally men of reason, right-thinking men whose ways of doing things defined the right way. Outside their circle they tended to look down on their fellows who could not boast of the pure, albeit fragile, Spanish bloodlines the Californios made much of and they viewed the Indians as miserable outcasts, fit for nothing. They embraced the interloping Americans and married their daughters provided they accepted the church and became citizens of Mexico, both conditions the earliest American settlers found easily acceptable.

The Californios were hardly as civic-minded as the Americans who followed them. But by rights, the governance of Los Angeles was their responsibility and they attended to it from time to time, maintaining second homes in the pueblo. The focus of their days was not Los Angeles, however, but rather their immense ranchos, their elaborate families and the equally elaborate families of their friends. The routine of that life was delineated by the necessities of the range. Cattle were birthed and branded and put to pasture and each year rounded up in events which involved the full physical and social resources of the community for weeks upon end. Beef was dried in strips and held in readiness for rich stews liberally spiced with native chilis, hides were tanned and shipped, fat was rendered into candles and soap. Betwixt and between, there was time for celebrations which, in the Spanish tradition, were not an adjunct to nor a break from more serious matters, but at the center of what life was about.

(Above)
José Ignacio del Valle on horseback at his rancho Camulos north of Los Angeles, ca. 1890. The land stretched for miles. The boundaries were hazy: a big rock, an odd-shaped tree. It hardly mattered.

What the well-dressed vaquero or ranch hand was supposed to have worn, ca. 1830.

The Lugo family outside their adobe in what is now the suburban community of Bell, ca. 1890. The Lugo family was a prominent one in the city's early history.

May Day at the Camulos ranch, ca. 1890. There was nothing like a holiday to turn out the family.

II

The Halcyon Years

The Mexicans thought they had been premeditatively invaded: the Americans were fighting to defend their honor. At the end of the war with Mexico (1846–1848), Los Angeles, and with it all of California, had been sheared off the Republic of Mexico and absorbed into the American dream of manifest destiny.

Such a seemingly momentous change underwhelmed the Californios. Those of Yankee descent, thoroughly assimilated unlike their counterparts in Spanish Texas, sought no independent republic. Nor were they particularly anxious to see California joined to the land of their birth. Californios of Spanish descent were likewise unenthused about being annexed to the United States. But, at the same time, they were, in affairs political, a long-suffering people, well used to the vicissitudes of rule by distant capitals. Washington looked to be not a mile closer than either Mexico City or Madrid. Matters were expected to continue as they were, no matter what. It was hard for Angelenos to think of change.

American designs on the territory came hardly as a surprise. Pio Pico, the governor of Alta California (the last Mexican governor as it turned out), had observed, in disbelief, Yankee "hoardes" pouring into the province. They were, in his view, an "astonishing" people who seemed intent on making things over as they would. Then, in 1842, an overzealous American naval commander, thinking war had been declared, sailed into Monterey, seized the city, and ran up Old Glory. He was informed by the resident American consul that no state of war ex-

"El Ranchito," the Whittier home of former California governor and Los Angeles luminary Pio Pico, as it appeared around the turn of the century. Pico admired the Americans, describing them as "adventurous voyagers spreading themselves far and wide over a country which seems to meet their taste . . . doing a thousand and one things which seem natural to them." One of which was erecting monuments.

isted and that Mexico was a country with which, at least superficially, America maintained cordial relationships. The flag was taken down. Apologies were offered. In 1846, formal war.

California acquiesced almost at once. A certain marine lieutenant, Archibald Gillespie, was appointed American military commander in the South, headquartered in Los Angeles. The appointment was an unfortunate one. Gillespie considered his troops victors and where there are victors so too must there be vanquished in which role Gillespie cast the compliant but not defeated Californios of Los Angeles, and so they were treated. Bristling with anger after multiple indignities, Los Angeles arose. Gillespie and his imprudent soldiers were surrounded on Fort Moore hill. Eventually, as their situation became obvious, they accepted an invitation to leave the city without further bloodshed provided they promise never to return.

But, war being war, the Americans did return. Andres Pico, brother of Pio, commanded locals in two glorious and not unsuccessful encounters with the Americans. But the tide of might was irresistible. At Campo La Cienega, Andres capitulated. His surrender signaled the settlement of the issue. California was, for better or worse, a part of America.

In 1848, the Gold Rush began. Prosperity for Southern California ranchos followed as they provided a good measure of the beef ravenously consumed in the northern mines. Los Angeles seemed destined to be the queen of the cow counties. Then, in the 1860s, a drought that proved disastrous for the cattle, the ranchos, and ultimately for the Californio culture.

Almost as disastrous were the procedures through which often lax Spanish methods of sizing land were converted to American legal titles. Language and legal barriers sunk not a few grand Californio families, their land finding its way into the hands of the lawyers hired to save it.

Los Angeles for the most part sat out the Civil War, local sentiment favoring the South. In matters of violence, of greater importance than distant battlefields was the mayhem endemic to city streets. Los Angeles, when it came to peace and quiet, was sorely tried. Successive waves of vigilante groups were sure the fault lay in not enough trials and not enough hangings. Lynch justice became commonplace and bred still more violence. In 1871, a wild rumor of a crime against a white man by a local Chinese spread and quick-tempered, self-righteous Angelenos besieged the Oriental quarter finally hanging a score of Angelenos whose only crime was that they happened to be Chinese.

In the 1870s, silver was discovered in the Panamint Mountains north and east of the city, and Los Angeles spurted ahead. A railroad, the first, had appeared in 1869, connecting downtown with the notoriously poor "harbor" at San Pedro. A newspaper began publishing, the water system was rationalized, social organizations were founded. Then, in 1876, Los Angeles became stopover on the transcontinental Southern Pacific. Soon guides and guide books to the west appeared. The city had become a place to go, because it had become a place to which you could get to.

Yet for all this, the Los Angeles of 1880 wasn't that different from that of 1850. There were about 4,000 souls when the city was newly American: thirty years later there weren't much more than 11,000. Yet those never doubted what was coming. "No man can fix a limit to the prosperity and greatness of this city in the future" bravely opinioned the *Star* in 1852.

Fort Street north from Temple Street, ca. 1869. At the end of its second decade of American jurisdiction, Los Angeles was a "city" of less than 5,000.

Looking north along Fort Street—later called Broadway—ca. 1869.

With the Americans approaching, the widow Avila gathered up her flock and fled the family's home on Olvera Street, leaving a hired boy to guard the property. Alas, the stirring sounds of military brass tempted the young guardian out to have a look. While he was gone, aides to Commodore Robert Stockton chanced by, saw the tasteful furnishings within, and at once requisitioned Avila Adobe as American headquarters. The building still stands on Olvera Street.

The Los Angeles plaza, probably in the 1860s. The structure at the center is a city reservoir. Across the way are the grand houses of the Californios and in the lower left-hand corner, the Church of Our Lady, Queen of the Angels.

(Below)
The Plaza about 15 years later. The reservoir is gone; the Church has been given a new bell tower. And Pico House, built by Pio Pico as the finest of hotels, dominates the scene. Immediately to the right is the Merced Theater (El Theatro Mercedes) named for the builder's wife. An inner corridor connected the second-floor theater directly with Pico House so that guests could pass between the two without fear of inclement sunshine.

(Top)
Hold-up re-enactment, ca. 1890. The stagecoach was the accepted mode of transportation. There were drawbacks beyond a rough ride, as dramatized here, drawbacks not always related to prospective immigrants. Major Ben Truman, a writer of thousands of words in praise of immigration, once lost a gold watch presented to him by Andrew Jackson. Truman failed to mention the incident in his sun-kissed panegyrics.

(Above Left)
Commercial Street in the early 1870s, known as Commercial Row in its earlier, less affluent days.

(Right)
The hanging of Lachenais, December 17, 1870. Los Angeles indulged in impromptu lynching. A Frenchman, Lachenais, angered that a certain Bell had stolen water from him, shot the offender in cold blood. Bell's body was located but not his assailant. Not until Lachenais, under the influence, commented on how foolish it was for the murderer of Bell to be sought far and wide. Wised-up vigilantes escorted Lachenais, no doubt sobered, to the corral of Tomlinson and Griffith at the corner of Temple and New High. And from there he took leave of Los Angeles.

Judge Robert Widney, a founder of the University of Southern California, organized the Spring and West Sixth Street Railroad, whose horse-drawn cars were the city's first answer to the problem of mass transit. In 1878, the line pictured here, which ran past the Plaza and Pico House, opened. It was a successful novelty and it only cost a dime, five tokens for a quarter.

Calle de Los Negros referred to those of dark olive complexion who'd once lived there. Americans literally translated the words, coming up with "Street of the Blacks," which prejudice transformed into an epithet: Nigger Alley. But it wasn't blacks who lived there, but the poor of Mexican descent and the city's Chinese population in what was Los Angeles' saloon and red light district.

(Right)
Chinese businesses on the Alley's east side, ca. 1871.

On the Alley's west side, the once-gracious Coronel adobe, the site of the death of a score of Chinese.

Water was a problem. There was enough, via the Los Angeles River, but not always in the right places. A system of *zanjas*, or ditches, were constructed to channel the fluid.

(Below Left)
The interior of the *zanja madre*, mother ditch, as it looked when workmen unexpectedly uncovered its remains in 1939.

In its last days, the wheel on the *zanja madre* at South Alameda Street.

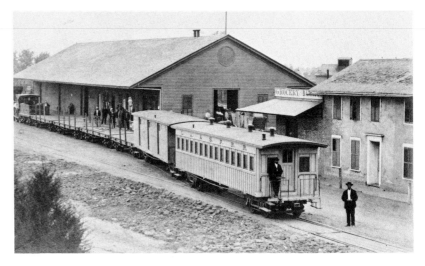

Pugnacious Phineas Banning never doubted the dismal bight at Wilmington would make a fine harbor. Freighters had to stand off shore, their cargos ferried to land by lighters, then transported by ox cart to Los Angeles. In 1869, Banning did what he could to expedite matters by building the Los Angeles and San Pedro Railroad, Los Angeles' first experience with rail transit.

(Top)
The train as it left Wilmington.

(Above)
As it pulled into the depot at Alameda and Commercial streets, downtown.

(Left)
In 1875, Los Angeles' second railroad arrived. John Jones created Santa Monica and to transport Los Angeles to the distant ocean, built the Los Angeles and Independence Railroad.

A round trip ticket to the shore and back was $1.00. The depot was on San Pedro Street, its most prominent features the two sphinxes which guarded the door. Just after the LA and I RR was absorbed by the Southern Pacific, one of the sphinxes mysteriously disappeared in the night. Later it turned up guarding the portals of the most fashionable bordello in town.

(Opposite Top)
It was thought a shame that there had been no celebration befitting the Glorious Fourth in Los Angeles for some years, a residue of the city's pro-Southern bias perhaps. In 1871, something was done. Businessmen shut their doors, festivities were planned, speeches were given. And the then volunteer fire department paraded past the corner of Temple and Main. It was accorded a great success.

(Right)
Los Angeles has always had its irregulars. In the 1870s, they were the Pikes: from whence they'd come no one was ever sure and fewer still took note of their leave-taking. "The true Pike . . . rarely follows steady industry," wrote an early observer. "He moves from place to place as the humor seizes him, and is generally an injury to his neighbors. He will not work regularly; but he has a tenacity of life." The Pike was an inevitable consequence of America encountering its sun-washed frontier.

III

The Boom of the Eighties

It was quiet. The big noise of the 1870s had been the steady clomp of the mule trains through downtown, trains loaded with silver ore from the Cerro Gordo mines in the Panamint Mountains. It had seemed in the 1850s that Los Angeles was destined to become cattle territory. Then it looked as if it would be mining. Now the mining was gone, the Cerro Gordo played out. It was quiet.

In the early 1880s, the stress was upon agriculture. The publicists told a disbelieving eastern United States God had provided such that the good Southern California soil would bear anything. Those actually here knew better: pests, disease, even the weather plagued farmers. Theodore Van Dyke captured it in quoting an old farmer on his love–hate affair with Southern California: "She is a tricky damsel, first-rate to flirt with, but of no account as a business partner. But I love her in spite of her tricks."

By the middle of the decade, the size of farms was increasing, the number of them as well. New arrivals were finding the claims to be truer than not. And then there were the tourists interested in the wealth invested in the climate. They came in winter and left at the start of summer which was universally considered by those unfamiliar with Los Angeles to be lit with the fires of hell. Nothing in the way of meteorological reports could persuade otherwise. Some, however, braved it. Those who came suffering from a plethora of diseases, chief among them tuberculosis, found the sunshine, crisp air and low humidity a prescribed godsend.

Then, in the spring of 1885, a curious phenomenon was

The melons, they said, grew so fast out in Southern California that you had to ride a horse alongside to harvest them. Slower-moving but no less sizable products of Los Angeles agriculture, pumpkins in the San Fernando Valley, ca. 1886.

noted. Many of the winter's tourists were observed to be still in Los Angeles. As spring melted into summer, new tourists continued to arrive. A certain buying and selling of real estate began. Prices, long stable, inched up.

In November of 1885, the first train of the Santa Fe line reached Los Angeles, a city which since 1876 had been dominated in rail transport by the octopus, the Southern Pacific. Immediately a freight and ticket war broke out between the two competing lines. Ticket prices plummeted in a furious determination to reach bottom. It was cheaper for locals traveling to, say, San Bernardino, to buy a ticket to Boston and just step off at home. Cynics suggested then, and have suggested since, that it was all very dramatic but all cleverly staged. No matter. It attracted attention to Southern California. Immigrant trains, special excursions and rock-bottom prices were offered from the East and Midwest to this Oz in distant California. And it was quickly clear that many were accepting the invitation. Before long a boom was underway.

Boom! A headlong rush of the new to get here and get a piece of this place; the first step in a dizzying round of buying, selling and buying again. An influx of sharpers and salesmen appeared ready to tract, plot, divide and subdivide. Prices lurched forward, senselessly spiraling up. An atmosphere was generated so thick contemporaries swore it could be drunk. And was drunk.

"I lived here in . . . an extraordinary year . . . in real estate matters," wrote Mark Twain. "The boom was something wonderful. Everybody bought, everybody sold . . . anything in the semblance of a town lot, no matter how situated, was salable." Twain was speaking not of Los Angeles, but of Hannibal. But he was speaking of all booms, everywhere in the West. Los Angeles happened to be one of the biggest and one of the last.

"It has been a subject of regret," wrote Charles Dudley Warner in the *Atlantic*, "that I did not buy Southern California when I was there last March and sell it the same month. I should have had enough left to pay my railroad fare back . . . and had money left to negotiate for one of the little states on the Atlantic coast."

In 1887, the boom broke but the bubble did not burst. There were those who lost in the decline of prices but it was hardly catastrophic for Los Angeles. Unlike many of the towns who had seen the boomer's hand, and had thereby suffered death when it was overplayed, Los Angeles still had its climate.

Boyle Heights and east Los Angeles, ca. 1885. It was beautiful, it was beautiful everywhere you looked.

From in front of the fashionable Pico House on the Plaza in downtown a party departs, ca. 1884. The four-horse "tally-ho" was the proper way to get about and a must for long trips into the countryside without which no visit to Los Angeles was complete.

(Below)
Colorado Boulevard in Pasadena, the mid-1880s. Pasadena contended with Los Angeles as an attraction for an outing, for dominance of the Southern California basin. Both cities were ceasing to be sleepy places at the far end of nowhere. Both were moving ahead and growing to resemble the towns new immigrants had left behind more than anything derivative of the area's Spanish heritage.

The McNally Home in Altadena in the late 1880s. Gentility, an Eastern sensibility, sprouted as easily as did the roses. To those back home, as amazing as the vision of familiarly dressed men and women and a familiar style of home in the midst of a supposedly barbarian land, was the sight of roses and snow-capped mountains in one photograph. The camera had to be lying.

(Below)
Los Angeles' first tennis club, 1884.

The town—it could hardly be called a city—of Los Angeles had acquired a rude elegance. Slight in numbers (not more than 15,000 by mid-decade), it was a cosmopolitan place from the beginning where, despite the dominance white Americans came to exercise, many cultures flourished.

(Opposite Top)
A Mexican adobe and a saloon in Sonoratown probably in the 1870s.

"Preacher" Johnson, a familiar sight on downtown streets.

Nicolas Martinez, "Marcos," in summer a vendor of ice cream, and in winter of hot tamales.

Packed carefully in their luggage, the Americans brought with them the idea of change. With characteristic hubris, they pronounced it progress. The arrival of first the Southern Pacific and then, in 1885, the Santa Fe, underscored how much change was coming and how important change was to be in a land which had previously seen little of it. The land was to be marked out, staked out, sold. Trees—and anything else in the way—were to be uprooted. Things would be different. Things would be better.

(Left)
The Southern Pacific's Arcade Depot at Fifth Street and Central Avenue, on land once owned by Yankee Californio William Wolfskill.

Bringing a palm tree to the Depot in 1888.

Life quickened after the Southern Pacific Railroad pushed through the San Fernando Mountains and, in 1876, linked Los Angeles via San Francisco with the East. Feisty Collis P. Huntington's line and the city made uneasy bedfellows. Before it had consented to build, the SP had extracted concessions likened by some to those requested by highwaymen. Wisely perhaps, the city had relented. After completion, merchants learned the SP intended to collect, "all the traffic would bear." In one moment of antagonism, Huntington threw his curse upon the city. He'd tear up the tracks and "make grass grow" in the streets. Until the second decade of the twentieth century, the railroad would be a force in city politics.

(Opposite Left)
Chinese laborers constructing the Southern Pacific around Bakersfield, ca. 1876.

Bridging the Arroyo Seco on behalf of the Santa Fe, ca. 1885.

The flood of the Los Angeles River in 1885–6 destroyed the Southern Pacific's Downey Street bridge.

Railroading in the days when the Southern Pacific merited a brass band.

—— ONCE AGAIN ——

THE LOS ANGELES IMPROVEMENT CO.

Places before the public another offering of those

BEAUTIFUL LOTS

ON THE HILLS WEST OF THE CITY.

(See Map Inside.)

THESE FINE LOTS

Overlook the City and the Ocean, and from them a most delightful view can be obtained.

A Cable Road runs Direct to the Property !

It is a fact that an investment in Real Estate on the line of or adjacent to a Cable Road in any growing City has been highly remunerative, and no doubt purchasers of this property will double or treble their investments in a short time.

GO AND LOOK AT THIS PROPERTY !

Make your selection and Mark your Catalogue before the day of the Sale,

Friday, May 14, 1886,

At 11 o'clock A. M.

Sale will take place on the Grounds.

The growth of the City is now surrounding this property with fine and cheerful Homes, Churches, Schools (public and private), Stores, and all conveniences abound, making this location one of the most desirable in the City.

(See Map Inside.)

To persons looking for either an

INVESTMENT OR A HOME,

WE COMMEND THIS PROPERTY.

Two Years' Credit !

TITLE PERFECT.

These Building Sites have advantages over other property in the city of Los Angeles.

ON THE HILLS !

AWAY FROM FLOODS !

Only Nine Minutes from the Heart of the City.

TWO CABLE RAILROADS RUNNING DIRECT.

Do not fail to examine this beautiful property before the day of sale, and remember

THE SALE IS POSITIVE.

(SEE MAP INSIDE)

Sale to be held on the Grounds,

FRIDAY, MAY 14th, 1886,

At 11 o'clock, A. M.

The boom was on. Overnight, land prices shot up, land agents appeared as if from nowhere. The eager and the innocent alike were induced with the irresistible offer of "a free ride and a free lunch."

The subdivisions marched like soldiers across the face of the basin, as far as the desert. The prospects trailed behind like camp followers. A promised future metropolis might be only a hotel or a school—if that. Improbably, impossibly large, no one stopped to question their isolated appearance on land where moments before there had been nothing but jack rabbits and chaparral. The brass bands, the warm beer, the cooling words of the spielers worked the trick. The problem wasn't sales, it was how to stack and count the money before the banks closed.

(Opposite Left)
An advertising brochure of 1886.

The Washington School at San Gabriel, 1888.

A barbeque typical of those at early land sales, n.d.

(Above)
The fashionable Mission Hotel in San Fernando, 1888.

The auction opening the Myrtle Avenue subdivision in Monrovia—and the ocean was very far away, ca. 1887.

The boom broke. Prospective immigrants were informed, however, in Los Angeles' eastern advertising, that no one had been harmed save the speculators. Los Angeles was still well, but characterized for the moment at least, by its dependence on agriculture.

(Left)
Ralph and Leland Kincade at the corner of Pico (a street then, a boulevard today) and Figueroa Street, ca. 1888.

Farming at the corner of Pico and Alvarado, 1885.

(Opposite Top)
Farming in the San Fernando Valley, ca. 1880s.

Rabbit hunts to destroy the pests which imperiled crops were frequent, ca. late 1880s.

By decade's end, Los Angeles' population doubled and then doubled again to over 50,000. The city was becoming a city. Then, in the midst of the Southern California garden, was planted the machine.

(Opposite Top)
In 1889, the cable car came to fashionable Boyle Heights, across the river from downtown Los Angeles.

The days of horse-powered transport were numbered. Columbia Avenue in Pasadena, in front of the Raymond Hotel, ca. 1887.

(Above)
In 1888, Los Angeles acquired its most impressive public building to date. A new City Hall was built on the east side of Broadway, between Second and Third streets. In both its interior and exterior it reminded one not at all of anything even vaguely native Southern Californian, but rather of life a continent away.

The tower in front of the Charles Hotel next to the prestigious Baker Block was a lighting mast. The Brush Electric Company convinced Los Angeles to erect seven similar installations at the cost of $1,000 each thereby making it one of the first cities lit, not by gas, but by that wonder of the age, electricity. It was considered a good promotion despite the fact there were those who were convinced the new marvel ill-suited female complexions.

Los Angeles from City Hall, ca. 1889. It was becoming a busy place, a place it was now possible to get up high in and see out over.

Third Street west of Spring, looking towards Bunker Hill, ca. 1888.

Santa Monica in the late 1880s. Now, a day at the beach involved traffic.

Central Park, later renamed Pershing Square, ca. 1888. Those left in the city enjoyed peace and quiet.

IV

The
Gay Nineties

The dust of the boom settled and, surprisingly, left no bitter residue. The real estate bubble had burst but little else. Los Angeles remained, slightly shaken, but, to hear its boosters, on course.

Residents of long standing now began to realize, not without discomfort, what the population swell of the 1880s meant. As perceptive contemporary Charles Dwight Willard put it, "Los Angeles had somehow suddenly changed from a very old city to a very young one." There was a pattern and Willard relished it: "Just as the Spaniards had wrenched the country away from the aboriginal tribes, and as the first Americans had succeeded in shouldering the Californios out of control of affairs, so now this overwhelming hoard of new arrivals took possession of the land and proceeded to make things over to their own taste."

The 1890s would be hailed as the last of the good times, the end of the quiet, simple times, etched in the memory of those who passed through the decade as the calm before the stormy twentieth century. It was the time the city realized, at last, it was a city. It was also a moment in which the city existed within and maintained, briefly, a delightful and human sense of scale.

But it was also a time of turbulence. A relentless, dull pounding echoed throughout the city, from the at first unheralded but ultimately spectacular discovery of oil man Edward Doheny to the steady tattoo of construction as the Port of Los Angeles took form at San Pedro. Only gradually did Los Angeles recognize the sound of massed, ghostly pile drivers, hammering down supports for a new Los Angeles and for a still newer Los Angeles to come, a city which was not content to await its moment silently, off-stage, but instead insisted on elbowing its way into being.

There was the struggle for a harbor. It is one of the supreme ironies of California history that two of her cities, San Francisco and San Diego, were gifted with magnificent harbors and yet in time would lose the contest for maritime supremacy to Los Angeles which possessed a coastal indentation which could only charitably be called an anchorage. Yet, by the turn of the century, Los Angeles' muscular boosterism had shoved down the efforts of the mighty Southern Pacific Railroad to locate the local port at Santa Monica. A handful of other competitors from Port Ballona (Playa del Rey) to Redondo Beach were likewise subdued and the federal government was ultimately convinced to expend the handsome sums necessary to transform San Pedro–Wilmington into the Port of Los Angeles, providing for the city what nature had rudely overlooked.

The trolley car appeared in Los Angeles, the electrified trolley which was clearly superior to the horse-drawn car and to the cable car as well. Next came consolidation, under the aegis of Henry Huntington who forged a network of intraurban "big red cars" in his Pacific Electric and the interurban yellow cars of the Los Angeles Railway. As the system grew, its nemesis, incongruously at first, drove into the scene: automobiles, which quickly stole the city's heart, turning it aside from a brief but intense flirtation with yet another mechanical marvel, the bicycle.

It was an age in which cities rose and fell according to the intensity and vigor of their boosterism, a lesson Los Angeles mastered. General Harrison Gray Otis of the *Los Angeles Times* spurred creation of a Chamber of Commerce and of a Merchants and Manufacturers Association, both to push for the greater glory of Los Angeles. Orange and lemon growers, the area's most vital industry, got the modern message of cooperation and product identification and formed a marketing agency which in time made all fruit not just citrus but "Sunkist."

The Pasadena Tournament of Roses was yet another spectacularly successful promotion. It passed from being a gathering of neighbors into an exhortation—well reported in the Eastern press—to all Americans to move west and make Pasadena their new home. Los Angeles countered with its own festival, La Fiesta de Los Flores, the festival of the flowers, or, simply, La Fiesta as it came to be known. Both cities well understood that nothing whetted the appetite of outsiders in colder climes more

than the thought of rivers of flower-drenched floats coursing through sun-filled streets in the dead of winter.

At the end of the decade, Los Angeles was satisfied with its labors, and well pleased that the population had doubled again, this time to more than 100,000. The future looked still more promising. More important, the future looked to have the same extraordinary lift to it that the 1890s had shown.

"California is new: there is nothing specially old about it," Los Angeles mayor, E.F. Spence, had remarked in 1891. Newness was important to the Los Angeles booster for without it, according to Spence, there could be "no hope . . . of its ultimate unparalleled prosperity." One had only to consider the ancient lands of the Bible to see that "the old and worthless" was "by the discriminating hand of a marching civilization" cast aside as "dross." There was, there could be, no dross about Los Angeles. Los Angeles harkened to the footsteps of marching civilization and fell in step. At the head of the parade.

Los Angeles was an American city and, as such, had its share of clubs, organizations, societies and associations, including: the Los Angeles Symphony Orchestra (1897), the Los Angeles Chapter of the American Railway Union (1893), the Vegetarian Society of Southern California (1894), and, the crowned king, the Chamber of Commerce (1891).

Spring Street from Temple, ca. 1892. Business meant routine: the same streets, the same tracks, dodging the same streetcars.

(Opposite)
A meeting of the Pomological Society at Pasadena, 1898.

An outing at Urbita Springs Park, n.d.

A meeting of the powerful Merchants and Manufacturers Association, 1897.

The question was not whether Los Angeles would get a full-scale harbor but where it would be. San Pedro was the city's candidate. Redondo Beach had deep water and was miles closer to San Francisco, queen of Pacific coastal trade. Santa Monica was closer still, but there the Southern Pacific controlled all approaches to a facility the railroad grandly christened Port Los Angeles. After a decade-long battle that reached the halls of Congress, the city triumphed. In 1899, from his office in Washington, President William McKinley pressed a button to trigger the dumping of the first rocks for the new breakwater. The machinery malfunctioned. Fearing Southern Pacific treachery, anxious Angelenos began construction by hand. Then they celebrated.

San Pedro in its still days, ca. 1894.

British ships unloading at Redondo Beach, 1895.

(Opposite)
The Santa Monica palisades, the approach to Port Los Angeles, 1894.

The celebration for San Pedro, 1899.

The Hastings ranch near Pasadena, 1898. Vines and vineyards were prominent features of early Los Angeles and, until late in the nineteenth century, Los Angeles was the wine capital of California.

But the orange formed the fess upon Los Angeles' escutcheon. The Spanish brought the first seeds. Don William Wolfskill, in 1877, shipped the first oranges back east. The trip took a month: the oranges arrived in fit shape. In 1873, L.C. Tibbetts of Riverside received from a friend in Washington D.C. two fragile specimens of the navel orange, imported from Brazil. It was a marriage made in an agronomist's heaven. The navel took hold in Southern California, and its success formed the basis of the citrus business

together with the lowly ladybug, imported to save the trees from a fatal scale in 1888. By the mid-1890s record shipments of lemons and oranges were leaving Southern California.

The picking, packing and shipment of oranges was less a family business than it appeared. After the organization of a Fruit Growers Exchange, growers had their orchards nursed and plucked for them. In 1903,

President Theodore Roosevelt helped transplant the first Tibbetts orange trees to in front of the Riverside Inn.

City life assumed form and, in this day, an economy of scale. Ease of access to transportation energized urban activity. A woman might board the streetcar in the morning and have it convey her on her day's errands. Her stops would include the stores where undoubtedly she was a familiar customer. Her coffee would be freshly ground, her meat carved to order. Laundry would be ready, bundled, and prepared to her husband's exacting specifications. And, as it had been in boom times so it continued to be in the '90s: there was business to do with the real estate agent. Only then would there be a spare moment in the afternoon for a stop at the ice cream parlor.

The Third Street streetcar, Santa Monica, ca. 1890.

Unidentified general store, Santa Monica, ca. 1895.

Unidentified butcher shop, Santa Monica, ca. 1895.

(Opposite)
Santa Monica Steam Laundry, 1895.

Real Estate office, Santa Monica, 1895.

Ice cream parlor, Santa Monica, 1895.

THE AUTOMOBILE

The first and only automobile or motorcycle ever seen in Los Angeles was invented, designed and built by Sam Sturgis & Bros., of West Fifth street. The second and third machines used in this city were also the invention of Sam Sturgis. The third one being a single seater built for a speed of forty miles an hour or even more. These horseless carriages are in a storage warehouse, where they were placed by a man named Eric, who was for awhile interested in them. He left the city while trying to take advantage of the inventor. Mr. Sturgis is now building a fourth model, as the first machines are in litigation, and the patents are tied up. It will be a month or more before Sturgis Bros. finish the new machine.

In the picture Sam Sturgis can be seen, dressed in black, with left foot on the machine. The motor in the picture is the second wagon made, and was a tallyho, which was tested in the presence of the editor of Wheeling. All the wagons are gasoline motors.

One of the foreign racing men at San Francisco has a motorcycle for pacing, which is run by a small motor burning oil.

The Associated Press is authority for the news of the adoption of electric motor carriages in this city for hacks, drays, etc., quite soon. Armour of Chicago is behind the scheme.

The electric motorcycle will hardly do for South California. Think of a trip from Los Angeles to San Diego. An electric automobile needs charging every six hours or less. Or a trip to Santa Barbara. Neither would be possible, as there are no electric power houses on the way. On the contrary, a gasoline motor carriage can obtain fuel at every country store.

Next week we will have an article on automobiles from the pen of one who has made a close study of motors. He will tell why electric carriages are inferior to other motors.

Wheeling half price to L.A.W. members.

The Spanish called the sticky goo which occasionally welled up from the ground *brea*. The Californios distilled it into kerosene, used it to seal the roofs of their adobes. But it was E.L. Doheny who realized it was congealed oil. Doheny, a mineral prospector, decided to take a flier and set about mining it as he knew how: with pick and shovel. When that effort had to be abandoned due to the overpowering odor of gas, a sharpened tree trunk was used as a primitive drill. At about one hundred and fifty feet below the surface, Doheny struck first gas, then oil. The mania spread rapidly throughout the residential heart of the city.

There had to be a use for all that oil. Sam Sturgis, bicycle mechanic, tinkerer, built the first automobile seen in Los Angeles and launched it from his West Fifth Street garage in 1897.

Early oil wells in a Los Angeles residential district, 1899.

(Opposite)
The decade was an age of fads. There was the Belgian hare craze—two years when no household was complete without a cage full of exotic rabbits. Then there was the bicycle, a phenomenon but a far more practical one. The eternal sun and endless vistas cried out for the quiet precision of the modern safety bicycle. Bicycling clubs proliferated. The bicycle was taken everywhere. By decade's end, there were more such machines in Los Angeles than in any other city in the world.

The popular East Side Club in Boyle Heights, ca. 1896.

The start of the Cycle Path to Santa Monica from downtown Los Angeles, around Washington Boulevard, ca. 1898.

An unidentified Victorian lady in her parlor.

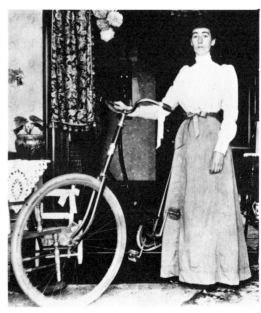

By bicycle, by slowly moving streetcars, by carriage or by foot, there were places to go.

Second Street, Pomona, ca. 1895–6.

On a picnic in Laurel Canyon, ca. 1895.

The boom time town of Willmore failed. As Long Beach, the city did much better and by the 1890s had a healthy reputation as a resort, ca. 1894.

Ocean Park, sandwiched between Santa Monica to the north and Venice to the south, likewise developed as an easy resort. Ocean Park, ca. 1894.

Professor Thaddeus S.C. Lowe was a man of achievement. In the Civil War, he invented the observation balloon and had the honor of serving in one, becoming the first human target in that conflict. In 1887, he retired to Los Angeles and almost immediately conceived the extraordinary idea of running a trolley up the sheer slope of Echo Mountain, outside Pasadena. The dream of building the world's first electrically operated incline railway appealed to Lowe. And he succeeded. At the summit was the Alpine Tavern, a hotel and an observatory as well. Lowe did it all, he said, so people could enjoy the spectacular view. Until its destruction by fire in the late 1930s, Mt. Lowe was a major tourist attraction.

(Opposite)
The twisting climb up the mountain was thrilling and spectacular.

(Above)
The car "Rubio" prepares to ascend Mt. Lowe.

In 1894, the sons of Phineas Banning, who had developed Wilmington and San Pedro, purchased the island of Santa Catalina. It was a picturesque enough place but as a business proposition it had never been made to pay. The Banning brothers proposed turning it into the Magic Isle, the Los Angeles Everyman and Everywoman resort.

The steamer "Cabrillo" left from San Pedro harbor. For those adventuring the night on the island and adverse to the creature comforts of the well-fitted Hotel St. Catherine, there were tent cities.

(Opposite)
Los Angeles heard the drums of war. The California 7th Regiment was mobilized and shipped out via San Bernardino, to the hails and huzzas of the crowd. No member of the infantry ever left the state, although a single battery of artillery made it as far as the Philippines.

A special funeral streetcar, decorated by the wives of railway conductors in honor of Conductor Ackerman, who had passed away of consumption. March 22, 1897.

Westlake Park as it appeared in 1889. "They saw improbable things happening," remarked Charles Dwight Willard of his fellow Angelenos who survived the 1880s with their good sense—and their fortunes—intact, "and they went on to expect the impossible." The boosters expected the city which emerged in the 1890s. They faced the decade confidently and had their expectations fulfilled.

V

Before the War

The years between the turn of the century and World War I were the confident years. It was the age, dimly perceived, of American empire. A continent had been conquered and all obstacles surmounted. Even as great a tragedy as the Civil War paled behind the beneficent glow of the Gilded Age. These were triumphant years, for America and especially for Los Angeles.

The Henry Huntington-organized Pacific Electric system continued laying track and expanding its service, dedicated to wrapping all of Southern California in a fixed-rail network. Fascination with the bicycle had peaked in the late 1890s but another mechanical marvel was harder to deny as a competitor to the streetcar: the automobile. And it was not long before yet another means of transportation appeared whose enthusiasts insisted would in time replace both autos and streetcars: the airplane. In 1910, Los Angeles hosted America's first air meet at Dominguez Hills in the southern part of the county. Monoplanes and blimps of every description flew gracefully through the skies easily convincing admiring crowds that the age of the air had dawned.

Movies were first shown in Los Angeles on a regular basis in about 1902. The motion picture industry was then based in New York City. Before long, immigrant movie makers discovered the ideal conditions present in Los Angeles and began shooting their short features here. As the industry took hold, it moved from downtown to remote areas like Culver City in the west and Toluca and Lankershim (later North Hollywood) north and west of

The small ocean front community of Redondo Beach stops to smile for the camera. Early in the century, rumors began circulating that traction magnate Henry Huntington planned on spending millions in the area. A frantic boomlet exploded, real estate activity shot up. But in good time, it was revealed that the rumors were entirely unfounded.

downtown, and to Hollywood itself.

City life became more elaborate. Golf was played on real golf courses. William Randolph Hearst started a major new, liberal newspaper, the *Los Angeles Examiner* in 1903. In fact by 1910, Los Angeles, with a population of slightly more than 300,000, supported five daily newspapers. A second high school had to be built (Polytechnic, in 1905). Abbot Kinney, visionary, laid out and constructed the most fantastic housing development the country had ever seen: Venice of America.

The city outgrew its nineteenth century form of government. The Southern Pacific Railroad's grip upon local politics, staggered by the loss of the fight over a new harbor, was dealt a final blow in the adoption in 1902–03, of a new city charter. Los Angeles proved an innovator by becoming the first American political entity ever to adopt initiative and referendum and the citizens' right of recall of elected officials, a measure created by Los Angeles physician and civic gadfly, Dr. John R. Haynes. In 1909, an aroused citizenry used the provision for the first time. Mayor Arthur Harper's grafting was a little too repugnant for the city, especially after cronies tried to steal the bed of the Los Angeles River for private purposes. At first Harper laughed at what the *Times* called the "grand bounce." but when it was clear the Harper regime was imperiled, Harper escaped through the technicality of resignation.

Los Angeles' budding labor movement supported the Harper recall and, in this, found itself opposed by General Harrison Gray Otis, the publisher/editor of the *Los Angeles Times*. The tensions between Otis and the unions steadily escalated and in 1910, a strike broke out at the newspaper. Months passed with both sides equally unyielding and equally resentful of the other. Finally, early on the morning of October 1, 1910, a dynamite blast rent the *Times'* printing plant, killing a score of scab laborers inside. It was the most stunning piece of politically inspired violence in the city's history.

If the *Times'* bombing was the nadir of the age, the completion of the Los Angeles aqueduct in 1913 was its high point. Water had always been a problem for the city. Authority over supply was first taken from private hands, a radical change in those days, and vested in a municipal authority. Chief engineer William Mulholland and others visualized a plan to transport the waters of the Owens River valley, some two hundred miles distant, to Los Angeles. It was an idea expressive of the age, a time whose accomplishments included the Panama Canal. Later chicanery and subterfuge would be alleged in the manner in which the aqueduct had been proposed and adopted.

None was needed: it was then a common belief that Los Angeles would get all the water it required.

For its own sake, Los Angeles was willing to stunt the Owens Valley. It was a decision in harmony with the political morality of the era which was founded in the firm belief that America meant the greatest good for the greatest number.

Complimentary was a form of civic cancer, a city expansionism common around the country. At the city's founding, its territory measured about 30 square miles. By the late 1890s, this had grown only to about 50 square miles. With the building of the harbor, the city doubled the territory under its jurisdiction. However, when Owens Valley water began to flow, Los Angeles was handed a mighty argument with which to convince smaller cities to abandon civic independence. Highland Park, University, Hollywood, Palms, San Fernando, West Gate, West Adams, Bairdstown, Owensmouth and more became neighborhoods of Los Angeles and, by 1920, the city spread out to an amazing 360 square miles.

If Los Angeles consumed Southern California, it was only too glad to consume itself. The annexation and growth of the period induced a kind of permanent civic self-surgery. Streets were constantly being laid down or torn up, repaired, widened, lengthened. Buildings were built to last: to last as long as nothing else was wanted and something inevitably was. In the special alchemy that applies to cities, this was a sure sign of success and Los Angeles began its twentieth century well pleased.

(Opposite)
In the wake of the bursting of the boom of the 80s, Los Angeles' finest promotional minds conceived La Fiesta. A yearly festival, it celebrated the sun and the flowers, and showed both to best advantage by being staged, and well-publicized, in mid-winter.

The guest of honor at La Fiesta in 1901 was President William McKinley. And why not? Los Angeles had voted overwhelmingly for McKinley, turning its back even upon native son Job Harriman. Harriman had run for vice president on a ticket headed by the man whose name was an anathema to the elite of the city: unionist Eugene V. Debs.

The Rampart Heights development, Third Street near Beverly Boulevard, 1905. The parade which most warmed the heart of Los Angeles, that around a new construction site.

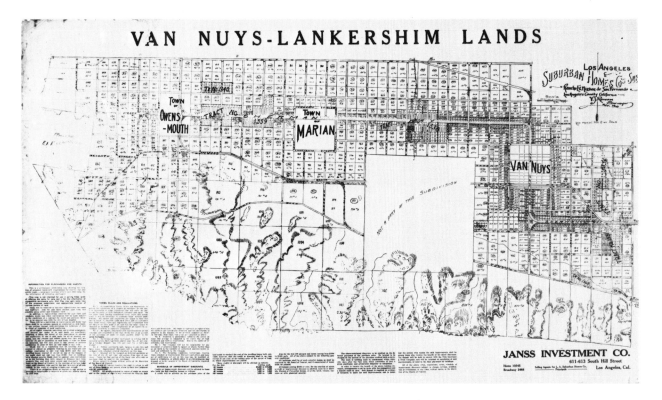

Realtor William May Garland's rosy predictions, displayed billboard size, were ubiquitous. In 1901, with population in the city only 102,000, Garland said that by 1910 it would triple. And so it had! Everyone believed his call for 1920 was too conservative. As it turned out, he was dead wrong, and population reached only 500,000. But who remembered?

Isaac Lankershim came to Los Angeles in 1869 and not long afterwards Isaac Newton Van Nuys arrived. Together the two men farmed on holdings which had once belonged to Andres Pico and before him to the good fathers of Mission San Fernando. The San Fernando valley it was called, and it was good for raising wheat. In the '80s, Lankershim land could be had for $65 an acre. That a home site very much less than an acre was going for "$350.00 up" a mere twenty years later is due to, well, inflation.

N NUYS   FEB. 9. 1911

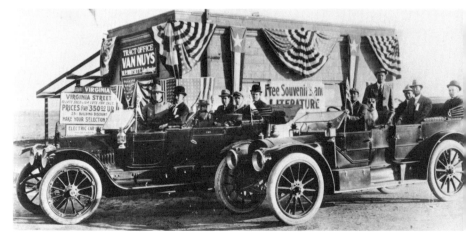

"All questions that relate to the general welfare of a country," noted the Chamber of Commerce's first secretary, Charles Dwight Willard, "are business matters." In other words, the business of Los Angeles was business. Seldom was a city growing to the prominence and importance of Los Angeles dominated by such a socially like-minded class of business leaders. So arose the Chamber of Commerce, in new headquarters, on Broadway, between First and Second streets. A not-so-subtle piece of one-upmanship which must have rankled the *Times'* General Otis appears on the *Herald*'s building. And at the Chamber's first annual banquet, walrus-mustached and contemplating the camera, is the General himself.

The interior of the Chamber building and its perpetual display of Southern California wealth. There were so many walnuts you could make an elephant out of them. "Don't imagine that it is an easy thing to find a soft job, a good pay, in Los Angeles," prospective immigrants were informed by the Chamber, as "Southern California is the Mecca for thousands who desire a mild climate." There was, however, a definite market for mechanics, laborers, and "men—and women—who are able to do anything a little better than the other fellow." And, showing the Chamber was right, is the busy central wholesale market.

William Mulholland arrived in Los Angeles in 1877. He was not formally trained as an engineer. He was an Irishman who knew how to wield a shovel. This skill found him employment as a *zanjero*. The *zanjeros* were hired to keep clear the ditches *(zanjas)* which distributed the city's water. Mulholland studied hard at night and one day became chief engineer on the huge Owens Valley project. Things happen just that way in Los Angeles.

It has been alleged that Los Angeles played the role of water vampire, stole the Owens Valley's water and left the valley to die. It cannot be said the city acted in an entirely saintly manner but politics then were generally less pristine than they are today. Los Angeles needed the water and, if it didn't exactly need it at once, it would need it eventually and that proved entirely correct.

(Opposite)
The construction of the aqueduct, ca. 1912.

Construction of an open lined canal in the Olancha Division, leading to Haiwee Reservoir, ca. 1911.

The moment the waters began to flow into the San Fernando valley, November 5, 1913.

(Left)
The north end of the Jawbone siphon, transporting water over the mountains, ca. 1950.

(Above)
William Mulholland, n.d.

By 1910, the presence of the automobile was firmly etched upon the consciousness of Angelenos, and by 1915, there were more than 55,000 vehicles at large. "Scorchers," feckless maniacs who insisted on driving at top speed, were the bane of biped existence and the city was forced to enact strict regulations. It was made a crime to exceed 30 mph anywhere in the city, 6 mph downtown. This made little sense to the motorists out where urban life seemed to end. And it was the auto which was helping to make those areas accessible.

(Opposite)
Sunset Boulevard at Micheltorena Street, September 1909.

A real estate subdivision being laid out along Sunset Boulevard in Hollywood, ca. 1905.

Cahuenga Pass in Hollywood, ca. 1910, as the Pacific Electric cuts streetcar tracks.

(Left)
Hollywood from Olive Hill, ca. 1909.

(Below)
Glendale Boulevard at Sunset, an early auto expedition, ca. 1904.

General Harrison Gray Otis had once been a printer but when the printers employed at his newspaper, the *Los Angeles Times*, asked to form a union, Otis angrily refused. Unions were combinations and combinations were detestable to men who nursed the myth that they'd lifted themselves to wealth and power by their own bootstraps. A strike ensued. Then, at 1:07 on the morning of October 1, 1910, a hideous blast rent the *Times'* Broadway printing plant, incinerating a score of nonunion printers working inside. Brothers John and James McNamara, national union leaders, were arrested and charged with having ordered a bomb to be set. Clarence Darrow was hired to defend the men assisted by Job Harriman, a popular young socialist and candidate for mayor. In Los Angeles, sympathy was with the McNamaras. That was

until they rose in court and admitted their guilt, apparently part of a deal for their lives. The union movement in Los Angeles collapsed over night. Harriman was defeated at the polls. And Ortie McManigal, who'd set the bomb, then turned state's evidence, was given a job as a janitor at City Hall and allowed to die in obscurity.

General Harrison Gray Otis.

James and John McNamara.

The McNamara defense team before the devastating turn of events: Job Harriman on the left; Clarence Darrow standing and Joseph Scott on the right together with the family of Ortie McManigal.

Los Angeles did not invent the airplane, but it did invent the air show. In 1910, at Dominguez Hills in southern Los Angeles county, America's first aerial expedition was staged and every notable pioneer of flight was there with the exception of the Wright Brothers themselves.

It was a magnificent sight, all those aircraft. Or it would have been: the photograph is a composite and not all these devices took to wing at one time. Dominguez Hills, 1910.

The aviator Parmalee in a modified Wright Brothers' design, at the second Dominguez Hills meet, 1912.

Henry Huntington was a master consolidator and, out of half-a-dozen early transit enterprises, the canny financier forged the Pacific Electric streetcar system. The intraurban "big red cars" and the yellow cars of the interurban Los Angeles Railways were ubiquitous. The "world's wonderland lines" the PE said of itself and it ran more cars than the transit systems of any other five major American cities combined.

(Opposite)
Glendale: the PE on Brand Boulevard, named for L.C. Brand who developed the area, n.d.

San Marino, at the interchange for Lamanda and Monrovia, ca. 1910.

(Above)
Henry Huntington at an employees' picnic, 1912.

The Trackless Trolley, an early electrified car system, ran up Laurel Canyon, ca. 1910.

Angel's Flight carried passengers from Third and Hill streets up nearly vertical Bunker Hill. Opened in 1901, it became a city landmark. Dismantled in the 1960s when the area was renewed, the city has yet to make good on a pledge to reassemble and install it.

There were places to go then. Join the crowds down at Chutes Park, Washington and Main. A thrilling ride down the slide and into the lake cost 10¢.

On Mission Road in East Los Angeles, just across the Los Angeles river, you could watch the alligators at the Alligator Farm take the slide.

It wasn't all crowds. Behind, around, the burgeoning city was the incredible natural beauty with which this place had been gifted. And there was time in which to enjoy it.

(Opposite)
The Los Angeles river as it flowed through Griffith Park.

The lagoon at the mouth of La Ballona creek, at the Pacific Ocean, now Playa del Rey, about 1902.

The New Garrick Theater, 1917. The hallmark of the age was the new mass entertainment of the movies. Crowds were called together by the newest release by a popular star—here comedian Roscoe "Fatty" Arbuckle.

There was time as well for less hurried amusements, time for lunch, al fresco, at Casa Verdugo in Glendale which had been transformed into a noted Mexican restaurant.

Change was of passing interest to the Californios. Their universe was ordered, stable and enduring. Americans were loathed to admit there was other than change. And order was always a *new* order. St. Athenasius Episcopal Church was one of the earliest such buildings in Los Angeles, having been erected in the early 1860s at the foot of Pound Cake Hill. In the late 1880s, the building was sold to the county, the eventual site of a new county courthouse. While waiting, the church was transformed into the offices of the County Assessor.

VI

Los Angeles in Color

The idea of color photography is as old as the idea of photography itself, although it proved a much more complex problem. The Frenchman, Joseph Niepce, who is generally credited as having been the first to take a photograph, was obsessed from the beginning with adding color to his work. He eventually joined another equally noted name in photographic history, Louis Jacques Daguerre, in a spirited, but ultimately unsuccessful, quest for a sharp, accurate color process.

Throughout the second half of the nineteenth century, amateurs and theoreticians with such imposing credentials as physicist James Clerk Maxwell contributed to the search for color photography. Success was granted a few. Perhaps the most remarkable instance was that of Baptist minister Levi Hill, who, at mid-century, demonstrated color photographs whose vibrancy was attested to by no less than Samuel F. B. Morse. Hill, remarkably, refused to share the secrets of his process and they went to the grave with him. Later some suggested that the photographs were the result of a fortuitous and unreproducible accident.

Good color photographs, the results of known techniques, date from the 1870s. These were complex and expensive procedures, certainly not readily accessible to the itinerant photographer out to document the passing scene, but rather restricted to commercial photographers working for fashionable magazines like the *National Geographic*. The technology for the engraving and printing of color photography proceeded apace of innovations in

Los Angeles needed a first-class harbor. Since one had not been provided naturally, it would have to be constructed with federal largess. The question was where. Most of the city favored the Wilmington/San Pedro area but politically powerful Southern Pacific preferred Santa Monica where it held all the surrounding land and could control all tonnage passing through. Congress, amazingly, backed the city, and on April 26, 1899, construction began.

FREE HARBOR
JUBILEE
Los Angeles
and
San Pedro.
APRIL 26 AND 27, 1899.
LOS ANGELES LITHO. CO.

"Where the Mountains Meet the Sea."

309:—Pleasure Pier from Palisades Park, Santa Monica, Calif.

The Pasadena Tournament of Roses began as a lark. Social notables in that most sociable of cities decided the New Year's season was, socially speaking, a disaster. What was needed was an event, and a parade with flowers was decided upon. The first Tournament of Roses was staged in 1890, hosted by the Valley Hunt Club.

By the turn of the century, the winter parade, now under the direction of the Pasadena Board of Trade, was good press. Parade sponsors decided to add the newest national fascination, college football, and invited the powerhouse University of Michigan Wolverines west to play Stanford. Michigan accepted and ungraciously stomped the Stanford team 49-0.

Of all the places along the coast familiar to Los Angeles tourists, the Palisades Park and the Santa Monica Pier ranked high. This was where seekers of beauty first encountered the ocean. Santa Monica had been established in 1876. By the mid-1890s, the trolleys of the Los Angeles Pacific line loaded up in downtown, passed through Colegrove (now Hollywood) and ended their runs by the surf.

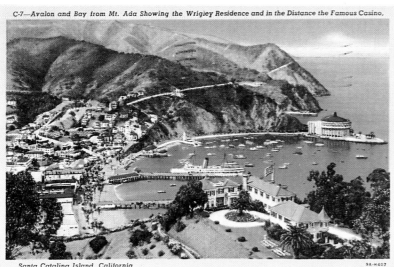

C-7—Avalon and Bay from Mt. Ada Showing the Wrigley Residence and in the Distance the Famous Casino.

Santa Catalina Island, California

9A-H407

Major William Rich Hutton was in his early twenties when he came west as paymaster, United States Army, New York Volunteers, during the war with Mexico. In civilian life, he had been a civil engineer. Fortunately for Los Angeles history, Hutton possessed some skill with pencil and brush and an inclination to record what he saw in his travels. He went up and down the coast, drawing Santa Barbara and Monterey, the missions and the presidios recently fallen to the Americans. And he drew what he saw in the little pueblo of Los Angeles. His pencil sketches give us some of our earliest looks at the city. His watercolor, reproduced here, is the earliest such work known.

The Banning Brothers purchased the island of Santa Catalina in the 1890s. In the early part of the new century, the Bannings sold out to chewing gum magnate William Wrigley. When asked how he planned to make it the poor Angelenos' summer resort, he replied: "Why, if I can get people to chew gum, I can get them to visit Catalina." Wrigley's most famous Catalina innovation was the Casino, a combination dance hall, restaurant and ornate movie theater. Here the famous big bands of the 1920s and 1930s held forth at elegant dances, with a 50¢ admission fee. It was a time when people sang of leaving their love in Avalon, knowing it was only a two-hour steamer trip away.

The Merchant and Manufacturers Association, the M and M, was formed in response to the bursting of the boom of the 1880s, as a device for the propagation of the faith. And the faith was Los Angeles. Harris Newmark in his autobiography (see bibliography) says it was the inspiration of M and M member Max Mayerberg to hold a carnival, to be called "La Fiesta de los Flores de Los Angeles." It was to be an annual city-wide event, designed to boost the city. In April of 1894, the first Fiesta was held. And it remained a tradition into the 1930s.

In the early 1920s, before the powerful International Olympic Committee, local real estate man William May Garland won for Los Angeles the right to host the 1932 Games, only the second time a summer Olympics had been awarded to the United States. First came the construction of a major stadium, the Coliseum, opened in 1923. But as 1932 neared, the city fretted. The Depression was on. Modesty wasn't just a watchword; it was a necessity. The centerpiece of conservation efforts was the idea of housing all the athletes together in one place. The idea of an "Olympic Village" was sold to a recalcitrant I.O.C., the darkness of the day forcing their acceptance of what was viewed as an intolerable break with tradition. Later the temporary village was dismantled and sold for a profit. The 10th Modern Games went on and were judged a complete success, the only ones in modern history to show a profit.

It's hard to think of Los Angeles without thinking of the aviation industry. But for most, that association stems from the World War II days when the modern aircraft giants emerged. In fact, aviation dates back almost to the days of the Wright Brothers. And with experimentation in flying came the idea of the air meet, the air show, of which Dominguez Hills in 1910 was the world's first. Air Fiesta was pure Los Angeles promotional pizzazz.
Sponsored by the Junior Chamber of Commerce, it featured the area's top pilots out to make an afternoon of it in Spanish costume. The public was invited to Mines Field (later Los Angeles International) in 1931. A band played, the planes were inspected and the pilots and their ladies and the pilots and their men played at being Californios. Then off took the machines on a brief flight north.

The shopping center at Third Street and Fairfax Avenue sat on land owned by the A. F. Gilmore family, land which at one time or another witnessed an oil field, a football stadium (later turned into CBS Television City), a drive-in theater, and Gilmore Field, long-time home of the baseball Hollywood Stars. In the Depression, it was suggested farmers be allowed to come to the area to set up stalls for their produce. In better times the market became a major tourist attraction and symbol of cornucopian Southern Caifornia.

The public was fascinated with flying and enthralled by the sight of the magnificent albeit flimsy creatures which took men into the air. In 1910, two sharp Los Angeles promoters organized America's first International Air Meet. All the greats were there: Glenn A. Curtiss who was the first to fly a heavier-than-air machine on the west coast, Knabenshue, an early experimenter with dirigibles, and Louis Paulhan. It was Paulhan who on the meet's second day scored the stunning feat of flying a biplane to the unheard of height of 4,165'. And then he established a new world's record by taking to the air and remaining aloft for slightly more than one hour, enough time to fly forty-five miles from Dominguez Field to Santa Anita racetrack and back via the harbor at San Pedro. The meet was not without tragedy. Art Hoxie, a local man, crashed in front of the grandstand and died. The Meet, repeated again in 1912, was a fitting introduction to the age of flight.

FIRST IN AMERICA
AVIATION MEET

LOS ANGELE

JANUAR
10-20
1910

American & Foreign
Aviators
DAILY FLIGHTS

Scene at VENICE, Cal.   8532.

Abbot Kinney was a true American eccentric. Born in New Jersey in 1850, he served in the Grant administration as a young man. Later he entered business and succeeded spectacularly in the manufacture of cigarettes. To restore failing health, Kinney came west, ending up in Southern California. Once here, he became a civic gadfly, a reformer, a man of causes. He aided Helen Hunt Jackson, author of *Ramona*, in her study of the plight of the former mission Indians. Kinney was also a builder. In 1885 he laid out a tract of land immediately south of Santa Monica, called it Ocean Park, and offered it as a prime resort. Then, at the turn of the century, he dreamed his grandest dream: a new development near Ocean Park to be called Venice-of-America. The plan was for a cottage-style development, the houses to be placed along canals, transportation to be by gondola, everything a doppelgänger of the real Venice. Even—and this was the point for Kinney—the cultural level of the residents. But as Venice was built it proved easier to import the gondoleers than it did the atmosphere of the doges. The renaissance Kinney expected from his Venice failed to materialize. Skeptics derided it as "Kinney's Folly." To survive, the development turned to roller coasters and fun zones, cotton candy and miniature trains. This new Venice survived, and slowly Abbot Kinney's brave new American Venice faded from memory.

In the 1930s' Depression, the Works Progress Administration's Fine Arts section commissioned Harry Biberman to do a mural in the Venice post office which fronted the Grand Canal, now filled in with concrete. The completed work captured exactly Venice lost and Venice gained.

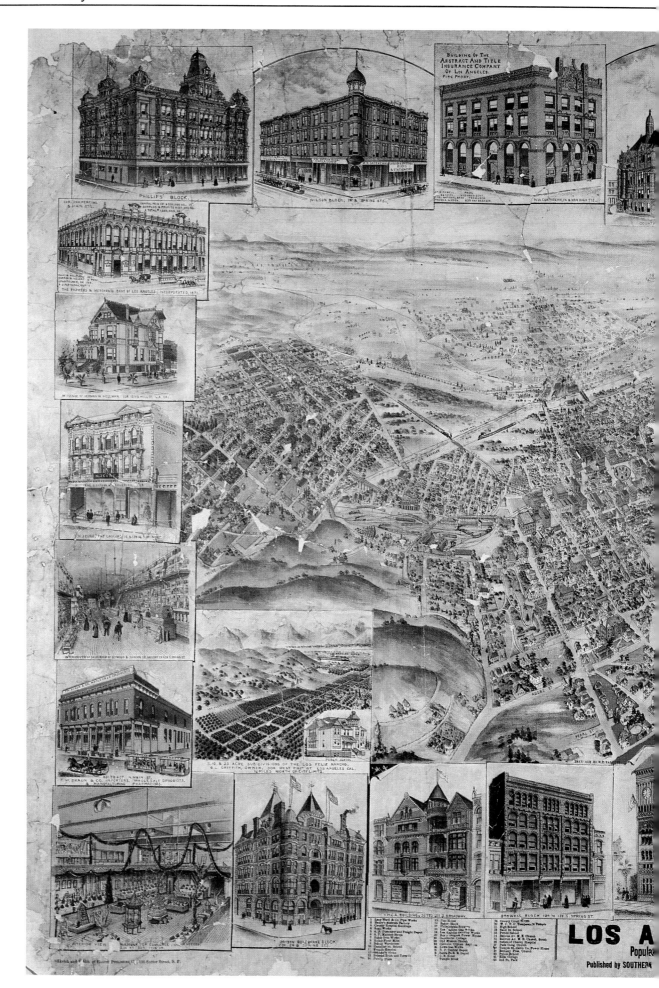

A bird's-eye view of Los Angeles in 1891. It was the best of times. The boom of the 1880s had burst but not the bubble. It rose in the air and glowed and Los Angeles stood amazed and proud of itself. "All kinds of people from all parts of the world," wrote a contemporary, "are coming to Southern California."

A tour around Los Angeles, circa 1940. First the strangest movie theater in the world, Grauman's Chinese. Built in 1927 on Hollywood Boulevard, it was of a day when movies weren't just something projected on a screen, but rather an experience. And the experience began outside. The Chinese's most famous feature was, and still is, its forecourt with concrete impressions of the stars, the inspiration of showman Sid Grauman. Next designer Albert C. Martin's May Company department store at the corner of Wilshire Boulevard and Fairfax Avenue, on the eastern boundary of Los Angeles' famed Miracle Mile. The May Company was an escapee of the Art Deco 1930s and, like the other great department stores of that era, it featured a parking lot tucked away in its rear, making its back door its main entrance. And to while away the rest of the day? Perfect! A football game at the Coliseum, the University of California at Berkeley against the University of Southern California. The score after one quarter was 0-0. Alas for local fans, Cal eventually triumphed, 20-7.

A bird's-eye view of Los Angeles, 1894. It was a fantastic city rising up out of a coastal plain and bounded by snow-capped mountains. Americans were sure they'd never seen anything like it before and were equally sure there could not be another such place anywhere in the world. Boosters played upon the theme of the land, its beauty, its promise, its curative values.

Artists also used the image of the land. As the city filled, land became an image reflecting inner turmoil—within the soul of the city, within the soul of its inhabitants. Two mural fantasies by the brilliant Los Angeles Fine Arts Squad, an ambitious group of young artists active in the 1960s and 1970s.

"Venice in the Snow" is an accurate depiction of the boardwalk which fronts the ocean in Venice with one addition: the usually placid elements have, in the eyes of the artists, been unleashed and the area lies deep in snow. The mural met an ironic and not untypical Los Angeles fate. While it still exists, a building has been built immediately adjacent to it.

The city of Sawtelle, a fanciful yet not untypical enticement for a development in the 1920s, abandoned civic independence and became West Los Angeles.

"Earthquake," (Santa Monica Boulevard and Butler in West Los Angeles) is an apocalyptic vision of a Los Angeles artery, broken and bleeding, the result of an earthquake.

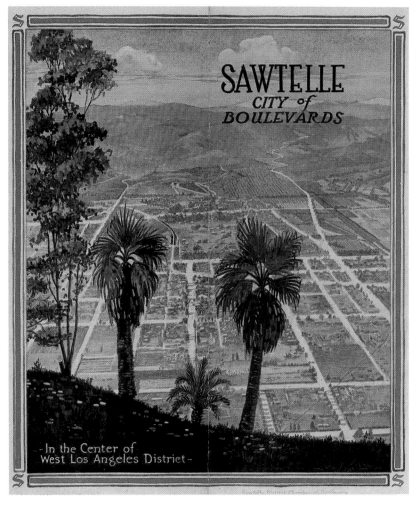

Downtown Los Angeles.

Century City.

A sunset downtown.

A sunset on the Pacific.

color film.

The jerky motion pictures of the day, always in black and white, aspired to color from their very beginning. Tinting was a familiar process. Whole sections of film would be passed through a bath and dyed a single hue meant to reflect the scene such as, dark blue for nighttime. This might be practiced as an art in itself or left "color" in name only. It was one of these pale imitations which eventually led to the development of true color film.

Leopold Godowsky, Jr. and Leopold Mannes were both the bright scions of musically renowned families and their early years were spent in movie houses until their lives took on a tone of parody of the standard Hollywood story. Not given to the making of serious music, they were instead drawn to the experimenter's bench. In the mid-1920s, working with very little equipment, they succeeded in their earliest breakthrough towards a practical color process. In the early 1930s, they were invited to join the Eastman Kodak Company where their work was proven, and in 1935, Kodak marketed Kodachrome, first in a form for motion picture cameras and a short time later in a 35mm roll film.

Kodachrome and other competing stocks suitable for use by rank amateurs enjoyed a brief popularity before the coming of the war. The government took Kodak's wartime production of color stock, but it returned to the market in the late 1940s and, by the 1950s, was economical and widely available.

It is a pity color came too late for Los Angeles or that in its experimental days the city was not photographed. (Ironic since Godowsky and Mannes lived and worked in Los Angeles.) If Los Angeles was the subject of color still film before the 1930s it has not been preserved. Yet this was the ideal spot. Commentators from Father Juan Crespi in the seventeenth century down to the immigrants thrown up as part of the boom of the 1920s remembered the city chiefly for its beautiful setting. The mountains, the liquid blue skies, the ocean, the endless sea of wildflowers which came regularly each fall and stayed throughout the winter and spring were photographed by millions of memories and stored. There was something else which intensified the vividness of Los Angeles in all its colors: the astonishing crispness of the air. That could never be photographed, just remembered. And experienced, for it has not entirely disappeared from the modern city.

In a view from Lookout Mountain, a November thundershower turns Los Angeles into an impressionistic cityscape.

VII

The Boom Twenties

World War I had not been much of an opportunity for Los Angeles. It had been fought inconveniently far away—too far for the city to have profitably served as a transshipment point. The war's materiel demands were not those which could be satisfied by Los Angeles manufacturers, of which there were few anyway, fewer than almost every other major city. Los Angeles, via its enlistees, garnered its share of patriotic gore but not much else. The war had not bestowed prosperity upon the city but the peace which followed more than made up for that.

The 1920s were to be an exceptional decade. It was announced as such, with Wagnerian solemnity, by the weather. In January of 1921, it snowed in Hollywood and the downfall was greeted with that amazement and glee which always accompany such periodic diversions from the norm. Later in the year, for the first time ever, the aurora borealis was seen over the city. In summer, Los Angeles experienced its hottest string of days in years, which did little to allay concern over a continuing, four-year-long drought. Then, in December, the drought lifted. The rains came and with them, predictably, floods.

It was the flood of people which graphically drove home the point that a new boom was underway. It was a flood which rose up in the city's train stations, coursed through the downtown real estate offices and banks before spreading out to lap in waves at every housing tract, cottage court or dream bungalow with a "for sale" sign in front. "Merchants and shopkeepers," wrote a contemporary, "roused from their solitude: they opened early in the

New York to Los Angeles and step on it. The first transcontinental auto trip entirely in high gear, 1923, with "Cannonball" Baker at the wheel.

morning and sold out before lunch. Doorbell ringers worked early and late, demanding the price of every home, and how soon the owner would move."

In 1919, 13,000 building permits worth $28,000,000 were issued. In 1923, 63,000 permits worth over $200,000,000 were granted. More than 140,000 new housing lots were offered in 1922–23. Assessed valuation jumped from under $650,000,000 in 1919–20 to over *two billion* by decade's end. In 1920, the city's population stood at just under one million, but, by 1930, it had skyrocketed to over 2,200,000. There was one good word to describe the bedlam that was Los Angeles in the 1920s and that was chaotic.

Everything which could disrupt a community now proceeded to happen. Oil was discovered: not just polite amounts but the richest strikes in American history. Beginning in Huntington Beach, following a ridge of geographic features towards Long Beach, then Signal Hill and nearby Santa Fe Springs, and as far north as Beverly Hills, the gushers appeared. The southern half of Los Angeles was torn out and replaced by the rudest of sprawling boom towns. The superhot oil industry produced a speculative mentality whose feverish intensity perfectly complimented the satanic temperatures being generated in the real estate markets. If it was the right time for reasonable investment, speculation both reasonable and rash, and not a little outright larceny were along and the line between these was difficult to precisely locate.

The 1920s were the age of pitch and con. The master of the financial three-ring circus was the redoubtable C.C. Julian whose folksy touch endeared him to the new Los Angeles masses. His oil pyramids and financial ledgerdemain on the stock market were daily newspaper fodder. Even the religious pages offered as much and it was in the 1920s that Los Angeles received its reputation as haven for the inspired and/or deranged of every persuasion. In truth, Southern California had been attracting the unorthodox at least since the 1850s when Mormons considered the area for settlement. No matter that, the 1920s saw irrepressible Aimee Semple McPherson with her God-given talent for theatricality both on and off the stage. More important and equally as entertaining to Angelenos was Aimee's archenemy, the Reverend "Fighting Bob" Shuler. From his pulpit at Trinity Methodist Church South, from his own private radio station, Fighting Bob preached the message of civic morality, sparing no names, omitting no details in sermons unmatched, saith his critics, in their gossip. Fighting Bob had enough impact to elect himself a mayor and be the decade's civic gadfly number one.

The success of Bob, of C.C. Julian and the others, demonstrated how powerful was the impact of the media. It was the golden age of the newspaper and at mid-decade there were six major dailies. And radio too, which broadcast a cascade of opinions by the far-sighted and short-brained alike.

There were prophets of gloom constantly predicting collapse, economic disaster and worse. There were those who had visions of Los Angeles at the edge of the world or those like Nathanael West who saw the end coming from impending, inescapable psychological implosion. Surely one way or the other it could not go on, not the gravy train, not the endless good times.

It ended on an October day in 1929 and not in Los Angeles at all, but in New York. It was over . . . but it was not all over. The speculators were hurt as were a good number of poorer folk who had been sucked into the dizzying play, although less was said of their fate. Los Angeles licked its few wounds and awaited the outcome.

Sunshine Acres Farm, outside of Santa Fe Springs, southern Los Angeles County, ca. 1927. The wildflowers were still here. But not for long.

The suburbs mushroomed as much or more than Los Angeles itself. Long Beach tripled its population between 1920 and 1930. Glendale, which in 1910 housed barely 2,700, was by 1930 home to more than 60,000. It was, for the moment, the fastest growing city in the United States.

Los Angeles was on the move. And it took along a house.

The automobile was ubiquitous. Between 1920 and 1930, the number of registered vehicles in the county grew from 160,000 to 842,000, about one for every 2.2 people. Everyone was going somewhere.

(Opposite)
Broadway at Seventh Street, ca. 1925. Sometimes it seemed everyone was going somewhere at once.

Studio publicity shot, 1929. The women liked anything mobile. Even trucks.

Venice, ca. 1929. Harold "Red" Grange, the greatest football player of his day, in Hollywood to make a movie, knew no man was complete without the right transportation.

(Top Left)
The opening of the Mulholland Highway, 1924.

A PE bus at the Beverly Hills Heights subdivision, 1925.

A motorcycle for the handicapped, 1925.

Delivering a Yellow Cab, a promotional stunt, 1927.

A delivery van for the Broadway Department Store, 1925.

It was obvious there were only four things you needed for survival within the city of Los Angeles. They were:

A gas station. The Gilmore station at the corner of Wilshire Boulevard and La Brea, ca. 1920.

A parking place. The corner of Spring, Main and Ninth streets in downtown Los Angeles, ca. 1922.

Another gas station or two. Texaco station on Wilshire Boulevard, ca. 1920. Violet Ray station, Hollywood, n.d.

And, last but not least, a car wash. The Western Auto Wash on Western Avenue, ca. 1922.

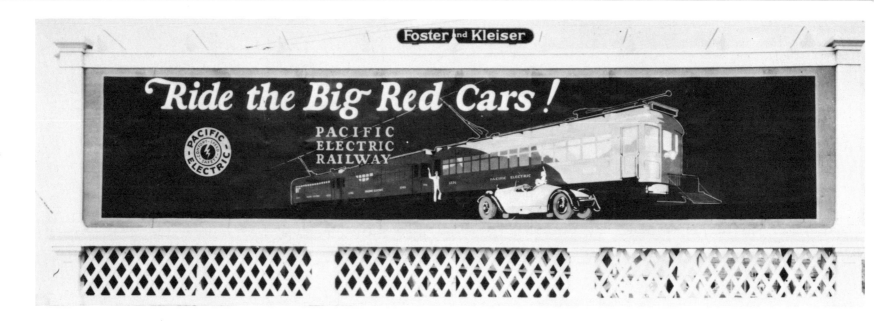

The alternatives to the auto were the "big red cars" of the Pacific Electric. The system appeared to be in good health but in truth, the handwriting on the wall for mass rapid transit appeared even before World War I. The system, at its peak, barely turned a profit. There were never enough riders and the company's answer was to cut service or raise fares both of which contributed to the attrition. Motorized transit, buses, began challenging the PE in 1915. As the contiguous cities began to gell into the urban mass of Los Angeles, the PE lost its one advantage: its own right of way along which it could conduct high-speed streetcars. The autos, like lemmings, threw themselves on the tracks spitefully impeding the PE's progress and the urban carnage was eventually insupportable. The Pacific Electric wasn't murdered. Just left to slowly struggle to death, unaided by both citizens and their civic leaders who had decided there would always be, in the land of the sun, endless numbers of cheaply operated automobiles.

A PE billboard, September, 1926.

"Hail the Motorman! He of Good Judgment; Quick Eye; Steady Nerve," wrote the PE in praise of the intrepid driver of its cars. The motorman had to have a quick eye and a steady nerve and in the end it wasn't enough. Streetcar–automobile clashes were commonplace.

The PE where it reached out to Beverly Hills, the Cañon Drive Station, 1925.

And south towards Long Beach, ca. 1920s.

The first PE subway car at the tunnel's north end, the Toluca Substation, 1925. Another irony: the PE's Great Hollywood Subway that went hardly anywhere at all. On the Hollywood line it ran from the Subway Terminal Building at 417 South Hill Street in downtown one mile north to Beverly and Glendale boulevards. The original idea, conceived just after the turn of the century, was a true subway to extend west from downtown to Vermont (the city's western limit) and from there to Hollywood, Beverly Hills and beyond. The energy and the civic commitment never materialized in sufficient degree. At its opening in 1925, the tunnel seemed to gape in mirth at its own short-coming.

In its earliest incarnation, the University of California at Los Angeles was known as lowly "Southern Campus," poor relation to its prestigious Northern cousin at Berkeley. By the 1920s, new and imposing buildings for what was to become one of the country's outstanding universities were rising on the city's western edge. "Sunset" the tract had been called early in the century. It had failed then but now was reborn, spectacularly as it proved, as Westwood.

(Opposite)
UCLA under construction, Royce Hall to the left, the Library immediately across the way, November, 1928.

The campus as it looked from the nearby fashionable Bel Air Country Club, May, 1933.

Westwood as it grew up with UCLA. Across the center, Westwood Boulevard, Wilshire Boulevard to the extreme right. September, 1929.

In 1916, Hollywood presented an epic, outdoor version of *Julius Caesar* with no less than Tyrone Power Sr. as Brutus. In 1918, the metaphysical pageant *Light of Asia* was similarly offered al fresco. Hollywood possessed a series of natural amphitheaters, perfect for art under the stars. In the 1920s, Mrs. Christine Wetherill Stevenson, patroness, mobilized the community which bought out a chicken ranch on the site of the proposed permanent installation to be called the Hollywood Bowl. It became the area's most famous landmark.

Between March and July, 1926, the Hollywood Bowl was given its familiar form.

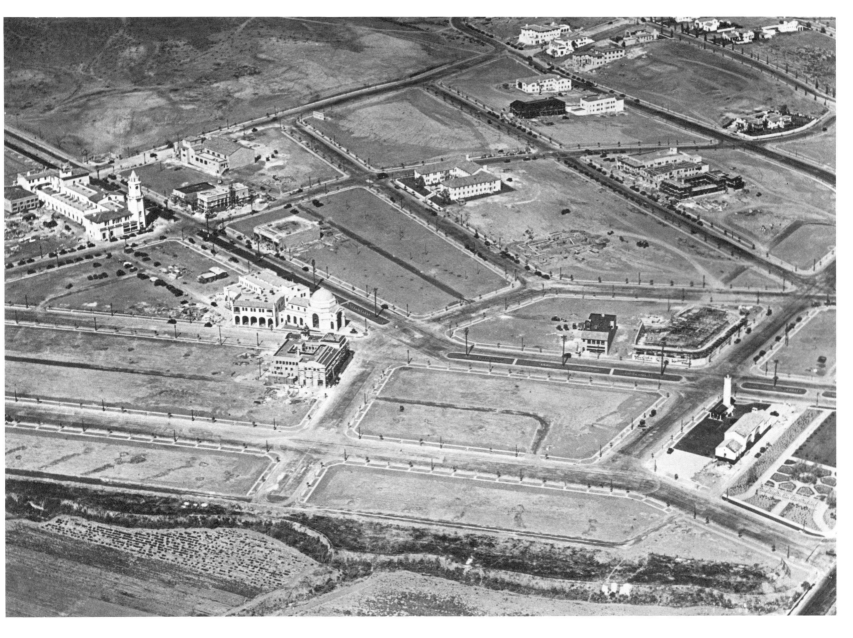

To enter a bank at the height of the land boom was to invite being accosted by an eager loan officer, out to lend you enough to get into that dream bungalow in Hollywood, that cottage in Owensmouth, that ocean view in the Huntington Palisades. And say! How about a few tickets to the Hollywood Bowl? On the house! And what was the name of your bank back home? Did you know your credit can be wired in a day? Money was cheap. Homes bought in the morning might be sold again at dusk. Whatever the temperature outside, the internal thermometer read more. "It is a daily occurrence which rouses no comment," remarked a contemporary, "to observe patrons of the soda fountains drop a five grain veronel tablet in their coca-cola . . . to brighten their spirits and divert their minds."

The Palos Verdes peninsula, 1924. Once isolated, now subdivision remade the land.

The San Marino tract, 1926. You could have it any way you wanted it.

The Riviera tract, 1927. A movie star's name was a sure-fire draw.

(Opposite)
The 1920s were the wonder age of Southern California architecture. If there ever was a distinctive local style, it was this, though it might not be here for long. For the motorist speeding down a sun-drenched boulevard, squinting against the ever-present glare, such "programmatic" buildings stood out, clearly announcing their purpose and inviting that brief pause which would surely refresh. It was architecture which succeeded in establishing planes in a landscape fused by light into an endless continuum of background–foreground.

Hoot Hoot I Scream, 1925. Now the Hoot Owl Cafe on Long Beach Boulevard, South Gate.

Unidentified ice cream cone, ca. mid-1920s.

The Tamale. Malted milks (as you like 'm) were the strongest potables available.

Mayor George Cryer presided over the boom times of the 1920s. His regime was hardly a model of political probity but neither did it empty the public coffers. And when it came to the construction of a new City Hall, Cryer decided to leave behind a monument in more ways than one. The city's most familiar symbol was executed with an economy Cryer personally oversaw.

His Honor Mayor George E. Cryer initiating airmail service with New York City, 1926.

And wielding the ceremonial shovel, ground breaking for the Mulholland Highway, 1924.

Finally the long awaited day: ground breaking for Los Angeles City Hall, 1926.

Los Angeles City Hall under construction, ca. 1927.

And at dedication, May 6, 1928.

Venice of America was the most wildly improbable of subdivisions and one of the few which took into account the unique characteristics of Southern California. The idea was to duplicate Venice, Italy: homes to be constructed around a network of canals which would serve as main arteries. It was the inspiration of Abbot Kinney, part philosopher, part developer and businessman. Kinney saw a community whose residents would obtain the enlightenment of citizens of Venice's illustrious namesake. Construction began in the first decade of the century. Alas, tidal action barely kept the canals clear and those who purchased homes overcoming what was then considered to be the great inconvenience of having an ocean nearby somehow lacked the sophistication of the age of the doges. Venice went into bankruptcy. Its salvation was eventually found in catering to the tawdrier demands of ocean-bound tourists. It became a roller-coaster-sideshow-weekend town. And if it was less than its founder had dreamed, still it was not without a character and charm of its own.

Venice, looking east from the Pacific Electric Station, on the edge of the Grand Lagoon, ca. 1920.

Bungalow on St. Marks Island, the intersection of Cabrillo Canal and Altair Canal, 1926.

Fireworks over the bathing lake at Venice, ca. 1920.

The original tract map for Venice, 1905.

Marathon dancing at Venice, ca. early 1920s. Jazz ruled the day: jazz sweet and jazz hot.

The police did their best to safeguard the town's morality. Jazz bred jazz morality and jazz morality was 100 proof and usually out of a bathtub. Meanwhile the force had its own problem with constant charges of corruption. In 1923, August Vollmer, the father of modern police science and then chief at Berkeley, accepted a one-year assignment to reorganize and hopefully scrub the force's face clean. He succeeded hardly at all. The status quo ante waited in the wings and, a month before the incorruptible Vollmer's term was to end (in September of 1924), billboards began appearing about town with an unmistakable message: "The First of September will be the Last of August."

(Opposite)
A Vollmer innovation: the first Los Angeles Police Department school, ca. 1924. Tenth from left is James Edgar "Two Gun" Davis, eventual police chief.

A LAPD raid, ca. early 1920s, and a captured still.

Where there's sin there's inevitably salvation or at least the hint of same. Aimee Semple McPherson hinted at both and her particular gospel was taken by many to be synonymous with that of Los Angeles.

(Opposite)
The interior of Sister Aimee's Four Square Gospel Church, ca. 1929.

Sister Aimee calls forth the faithful and the doubters as well, ca. 1930.

The Four Square Gospel Church as it appeared in 1929. It still stands on Glendale Boulevard near Sunset in the Echo Park district.

If Los Angeles lacked a reputation for moral perfection her fame for hospitality was unblemished. As the tide of immigration increased, state societies appeared which held annual, even semiannual, picnics designed to keep the home folks in touch. Some state societies were so swollen they broke down into county units.

(Above)
The Marion County, Iowa, annual picnic at Sycamore Grove in the Arroyo Seco, 1929.

Hospitality of a different sort and definitely not for the home folks.
(Right)
Interior of a private banquet room at the Cafe Montmartre, Sunset Boulevard, 1929. Tenth from left—it's her party—is gossip columnist Louella Parsons.

It was something of a joke. Los Angeles, they'd said in the mid-nineteenth century, had no future for it had no nearby sources of energy. In 1892, E.L. Doheny struck oil in the center of the city. In 1920, oil was discovered at Huntington Beach, just outside Los Angeles county. Then experts noticed Signal Hill. Before the war, Signal Hill had been subdivided. The development had not fared well but there were enough houses in place to dissuade one oil company from exploring. Royal Dutch Shell had no such hesitations and their subsequent strike on Signal Hill proved one of the richest in American history. Soon gushers were spread like wildflowers. In 1917, Los Angeles had produced just over 3,000,000 barrels of oil. In 1923, it produced just over 157,000,000 barrels. Everybody wanted in. Everybody wanted a share.

(Opposite)
Oil well at the corner of Orange and Garvey avenues in suburban Monterey Park. In 1927, oil was discovered under the real estate office of L.H. Browning and soon the L.H. Browning Oil Well No. 1 had arisen.

Sales of oil shares in L.H. Browning No. 1, Monterey Park, 1927. Fortunes were not merely, nor solely, made pumping oil. Selling shares increased the return.

Union Oil Company well, Signal Hill, 1925. The gushers were everywhere. The companies gave up bothering to contest damage claims of those caught in the black showers.

Signal Hill as it appeared before oil, ca. 1920.

Signal Hill, as the oil flowed, ca. 1925.

Crowds. Los Angeles had become a city of crowds. The fields that characterized the city—the long, seemingly endless fields of poppies and goldenrod which stretched west towards the ocean or east towards the mountains—were still there but each year were growing fainter. Disappearing under the crowds.

An unidentified strike, Los Angeles, ca. 1926.

The Beverly Hills Women's Club, ca. 1929.

Of course, no single generalization is true. It was also a city in which one could be alone or with a few friends. That it possessed the crowds and yet the solitude was perhaps its greatest strength.

Sailors on leave on the Municipal Pier at Long Beach, 1925.

The Old Soldiers' Home at Sawtelle, now part of West Los Angeles, ca. 1926.

VIII

The Depression Decade

There'd been a riot down at the Spring Street head-quarters of the Pacific Coast Stock Exchange in early 1927. Trading had suddenly been suspended in Julian Petro-leum. "Julian Pete" it was affectionately known to thousands of little-guy stockholders for whom it was as quintessentially Los Angeles as oranges, and just as golden. Created by folksy, compelling conman C.C. Julian, stirred by even more vicious hands when C.C. bowed out, the fall of Pete uncovered as ugly a fiduciary daisy chain as Los Angeles had ever seen. The year 1927 held a foretaste of what 1929 and Black Friday would be.

Stock market transactions on the Los Angeles Exchange rose in 1927–28. But reality finally caught up with the market and averages plummeted. They fell steadily and kept on falling right past the bad news from New York until an all-time low was established, a low a mere four percent of the high posted in the decade of the 1920s. The value of manufactures, assessed valuation and every other indicator fell about as sharply, an apt portrait of the economic doldrums that settled upon America in the 1930s.

But as the news of economic and agricultural disaster deepened, Los Angeles realized its Depression was bleak, but not getting bleaker. Matters were still, but they had not stagnated. In part, it was because the Depression was slow in affecting the motion picture industry. Los Angeles, too, had a tradition of weathering economic storms and the pattern repeated.

As the closures, the unemployment, the bread lines, the wandering bands of vagabonds were slow in coming,

Rolling Hills estates, on the Palos Verdes peninsula neighboring the harbor at San Pedro, 1937. "Country Life–City Convenience" although in the Depression, even Los Angeles had to stop and ask itself what were the conveniences of the city.

immigration to Southern California continued. But the newcomers were no longer the awe-struck tourists and the eager retirees, pockets bulging with cash, ready to invest. The newcomers now were those fleeing horrors elsewhere and coming, as often as not, without the cash in hand for their next meal. The city, to its shame, took up the welcome mat.

Resident Mexicans, including American citizens of Latin extraction, were rounded up by the authorities, herded aboard trains and shipped like cattle back across the border. The city figured up the cost of food payments and decided it was cheaper to accept the cut rates the railroads were offering and solve the problem of the out-of-work and hungry by getting rid of them. Those the city could not get rid of, it tried to keep out. The Los Angeles Police Department posted officers at the Arizona border, hours away from the city, forming what was called the "bum blockade." Cars were illegally detained, their occupants inspected and those attempting to enter the state without what was thought to be sufficient funds turned away.

The decade of the 1930s offered those within the city much for their amusement and occasional edification. A civic sideshow was convened. Self-improvement societies, good-cheer clubs and pseudo-intellectual associations of every size and variety blossomed forth. Their most favorite meeting grounds were the city's cafeterias where a good, cheap meal was to be had. In the case of Clifton's Cafeterias, the "cafeterias of the golden rule," all a patron had to do was decline to pay his bill for whatever reason and he was not charged.

How to change the world was a constant subject of conversation: politics offered excitation and diversion. Conservatives in Los Angeles and around the state blanched in horror as socialist, author and essayist, Upton Sinclair, announced for the governorship on what he called the E.P.I.C., or End Poverty in California, platform. He was no fringe candidate to be whistled away and it was only by the skin of their teeth, and not without questionable tactics, that the status quo defeated the Sinclair bandwagon. Its demise birthed a half-hundred other schemes, each more flamboyant and unrealistic than the last. Ham and Eggs, Thirty Dollars every Thursday and the Townsend Plan were genuine expressions of social pain, of social dislocation. They were also movements which became crusades and crusades which became the personal fiefs of unscrupulous organizers.

On the local level, city government continued as great a source of mirth as ever. A succession of police "spy squads" worked on behalf of various mayors though to what end was never exactly clear. But they were joyous good news for the newspapers who took to lambasting administration after administration and who had little trouble, along the way, citing chapter and verse of the corruption rampant among the guardians of law and order. It was the darkest decade the police force had known.

In 1932, Frank Shaw, a former city councilman, assumed the mayor's chair. In a corner office was installed the mayor's brother, Joe Shaw, to whom, it was widely believed, one had to talk and talk seriously if the matter involved the city and its business. Despite the exposés and the reformers, things continued as they always had. That was, until the middle of the decade when a new reform movement began to appear, and in 1938, after a bitter campaign, the Shaw administration was recalled, and a truly reform-minded alternative installed in office. The gravy train down at City Hall was derailed.

By then, matters were improving for the city as a whole. Business had started to revive. It took a war to renew the city as eventually proved true for the entire country. But that did not stop the old timers from their belief that the deity or at least a very special and benign providence looked after Los Angeles. The Depression not withstanding, they held, the '30s hadn't been half bad.

One city convenience was the bread line which, even in ever-prosperous Los Angeles, garnered, in 1938, an increasingly (albeit formerly) affluent crowd.

There were still posh accommodations for dining though it cannot be said that Los Angeles was known for the quality of its food. Before World War I, social critic Willard Huntington Wright had dispensed with Los Angeles cuisine as easily as he dispensed with the city in general: "The average resident of Los Angeles has an ingrained suspicion of ornamental and extravagant cooking. He prefers the good old dishes and the homely nomenclature." But if Los Angeles did not dine well, it dined in style: no city matched the exuberance of restaurant styling here.

(Opposite)
King's Tropical Inn, "Squab dinners—.90," 5879 West Washington Boulevard, Culver City, 1937.

The ubiquitous drive-in, Simons, at the intersection of Wilshire Boulevard and Fairfax, ca. 1937.

The Brown Derby at 3427 Wilshire Boulevard, ca. 1937.

Interior of the Club Versailles, Santa Monica, 1938. If you had the wherewithal, why not pass the Depression away in comfortable surroundings?

Health faddists in Hollywood, ca. 1930. If times were bad, at least keeping healthy also had the effect of keeping busy.

Health Water Center, 1521 N. Vine Street, Hollywood, ca. 1930.

(Opposite)
A Works Progress Administration sewer project, Alameda Street at 41st Place, June, 1937. What really mattered was a job. Any job. Working put food on the table.

The sewer detail, Los Angeles Department of Public Works, ca. 1935.

Los Angeles County Charities Food Exchange, ca. 1930. The poor ate where they could, and through the generosity of others.

Antonio Cornero Stralla, Tony Cornero they called him, the "admiral of the rolling bones," was fleet commander of the strangest flotilla never to set sail. The idea had been around since the late 1920s: outfit an old barge with slot machines and crap tables, float her three miles off the Southern California coast where state authorities had no jurisdiction and the Feds no law against gambling, and sit back and rake it in. Cornero, an importer of quality liquors in the days when there were laws against same, went one better. He outfitted his "Rex" as a luxury casino, stripped the grime off visiting the ships, and advertised his as a middle-class attraction. He was wildly successful. Cornero had had scraps with the law which were all, from the law's point of view, unsatisfactory. Then, in 1939, Attorney General Earl Warren launched a new assault. In lightning raids, the fleet of gambling ships were seized. But not the "Rex" nor Cornero who, high-pressure fire hose in hand, held the force of the law at bay in the bay. The standoff quickly became a comic opera contretemps the newspapers delightedly tagged "the Battle of Santa Monica Bay." After a week, Cornero surrendered. He had everything aboard, he told the press, save for a barber and he needed a haircut. Acting on dubious legal grounds, the gaming equipment of the "Rex" and other ships was seized and destroyed. By the time the matter got to the courts, the era of the gambling ships was over. War had been declared and nobody was about to roll dice with the Japanese.

The police were corrupt, it was generally conceded, when it came to the enforcement of the vice laws. Bookmaking, gambling and prostitution were nowhere hard to come by. The politicians were more annoyed at the frequent vice exposés in the reform newspapers. Their relationship with the city's homegrown Anglo-Saxon criminal syndicate was of long standing and renewed at election time. The businessmen seemed not to care. Perhaps because nothing was viewed as inappropriate as long as it didn't darken the city's name too severely or cut into the tourist trade.

(Above)
The Los Angeles Police Department annual parade, 1938.

(Opposite)
The Pasadena Police Department Pistol Team, ca. 1930. When it came to trick shooting, however, Los Angeles held the championship.

Deputy Police Chief James Edgar "Two Gun" Davis, 1930, holding the trophy won by the LAPD's pistol team.

Roy "Strong Arm Dick" Steckel, chief, LAPD, 1929–33 with James Edgar Davis, chief, 1926–29 and 1933–38.

County Jailer Clem Peoples with Los Angeles County Sheriff Eugene Biscailuz, ca. 1936.

(Above)
The sun and the shows were free. Pasadena's famous Tournament of Roses expresses something quintessentially American. So it must have seemed to Professor Albert Einstein, who found himself at the center of one of America's frequent maelstroms of hero worship. Visiting Cal Tech in Pasadena in 1932, Einstein must have been amazed to find $E = MC^2$—done in flowers.

Los Angeles had won the right to host the 1932 Olympics but that had been in the boom days of the 1920s. By the early 1930s, the Depression was on. Los Angeles forged ahead with Spartan games, making do, and it did so brilliantly. The athletes provided a spirited contest and the Summer Games were a complete success.

(Center)
Opening day at the 10th Modern Olympiad, July 30, 1932.

Vice President Charles Dawes substituted for President Herbert Hoover, then locked in a reelection struggle he eventually lost.

The Olympic Village—Los Angeles had dreamed up the idea for economy's sake. At the conclusion of the Games, the clapboard houses on a plain in Baldwin Hills were torn down and sold for scrap.

Harry Chandler, who succeeded the crusty General Otis as publisher and guiding light of the *Los Angeles Times*, had never been pleased with the colorful, he would have said too colorful, old Chinatown which sprawled near the Plaza downtown. What would better serve the scenery would be a train station, despite the fact it was not the facility the railroads had in mind. When it came to matters of downtown geography, Harry Chandler usually had his way. Chinatown was renewed out of

existence. In its place arose, in 1939, Union Station. The Chinese were relocated north and east to two new "Chinatowns" built with the sanitary requirements of the tourist trade in mind. China City was one, every occidental's view of what China should be. It burned down about a year after construction.

Downtown Los Angeles with its Chinatown, 1933.

Downtown Los Angeles minus its Chinatown, 1935.

Downtown Los Angeles' Union Station, ca. 1939.

Tourist attraction China City, ca. 1938.

Colonel Griffith J. Griffith donated the sprawling park which bears his name. Sixteen years after his original beneficence, the eccentric Colonel decided what Mount Hollywood—the highest point in his park—needed was an observatory. To this end he gave $100,000.

Griffith Planetarium under construction, ca. 1933.

Griffith Planetarium, ca. 1934.

Disaster plagued Los Angeles in the 1930s. It rained as it seldom had before and major floods in 1934 and 1938 resulted from downpours of as much as ten inches in a few hours. When the earth was not sodden, it was being shaken. A major earthquake struck southern Los Angeles county, around Long Beach and Compton, in 1933. And then there were fires.

Compton Boulevard in Compton shows the effect of the earthquake on brick buildings, March, 1933.

In Long Beach, the devastation was as great.

In 1938, the historical Baker Block, built in the 1870s, was damaged by fire.

The Salvation Army set up tent cities to feed and house the homeless.

(Opposite)
Flood damage along the Los Angeles River, 1938.

In 1934–35, floods drove thousands from their homes in Long Beach.

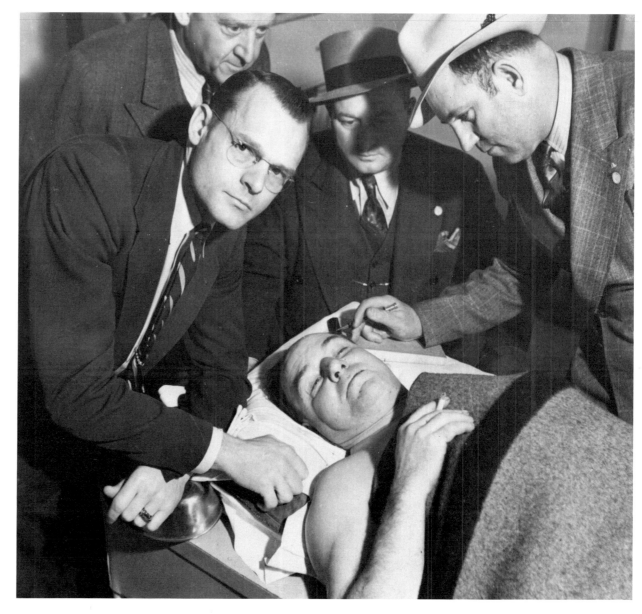

The sideshow of the decade was the City Hall Follies of 1938. "Hiz honner da mayor," Frank Shaw, was no less—nor more—than the chief executives who had preceded him. Either they were unusually dense or they took care not to inquire too closely into certain practices of their closest advisers. The reformers, as usual, screamed. After a stint on a grand jury, restaurateur Clifford Clinton became convinced vice was protected in Los Angeles and that the trail led to the mayor's office. Still, nothing might well have happened had not detective Harry Raymond, of questionable probity himself, been blown up trying to start his car. Raymond survived. His bombers turned out to be members of a secret police "spy squad," charged with subverting those accused of antimayor activities. Clinton and his band launched a recall movement. Soon the radio was crackling with charge and counter-charge, airplanes appeared dropping outrageous propaganda. When it was over, Frank Shaw had been recalled from office and a reform administration swept in.

(Opposite)
William Andrews Clark, benefactor of the Los Angeles Philharmonic, gifted the city with a statue of Beethoven in Pershing Square. Mayor Shaw (center) planted a tree. On the left is Philharmonic conductor Otto Klemperer.

Shaw had to give up at least one step to his police chief, James Edgar "Two-Gun" Davis. In uniform, Davis and, next to him, Mayor Shaw.

Harry Raymond was sniffing out pay-offs. Until the morning someone connected a bomb to his car. On stretcher, Raymond; with glasses, Clifford Clinton.

(Top Right)
Clifford Clinton had his fingers firmly on the Southern California pulse. He knew that the way to recall a mayor was to send out the girls.

Mayor Shaw tried to tough it out. His smile grew progressively weaker.

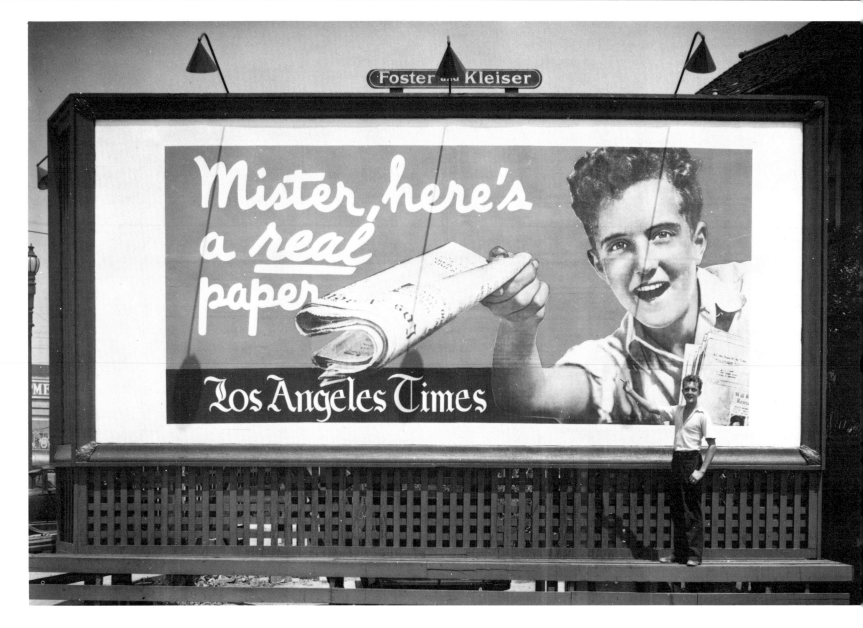

For the better part of the 1930s, Los Angeles had five major daily newspapers contending for public favor. They were no longer as adamantly opposed to one another's styles and political views as they'd once been, yet between them were real differences.

Harrison Gray Otis elevated the *Los Angeles Times*, between the 1880s and 1914, into the city's widest-read newspaper and into his personal mouthpiece. Son-in-law Harry Chandler continued the Otis tradition, and the Otis style. Hardly admired by professional newsmen, Chandler cared not a wit. In Los Angeles the *Times*' voice was *heard*.

(Opposite)
Billboard advertisement for the *Times*, ca. 1935.

Harry Chandler locks the doors to the *Times*' Spring Street headquarters, son Norman looks on.

The *Times*' most colorful competitor was Elias Manchester Boddy and his *Daily News*. The *Daily News* had been founded as a tabloid by Cornelius Vanderbilt, Jr. but without the mix of sex and sensationalism associated with tabloid style. By the late 1920s, Vanderbilt's "experiment" had failed and Boddy was brought in to revive the newspaper. He proved ever shrewd and occasionally brilliant. In came a little more sex—not enough to really offend moralistic Los Angeles—and a lot more scandal. The *Daily News* crusaded and occasionally, at Boddy's direction, tilted, as when its publisher took up the obscure idea of technocracy and elevated it, in a few lengthy pieces, to the status of a cause. And then just as quickly dropped it.

(Top Right)
Manchester Boddy in the printing plant of the *News*.

The *News* Building at 123 East Pico, ca. late 1920s.

Abbot Kinney's grand idea, Venice of America, had, by the 1920s, been given the status of an amusement zone. In 1925, it surrendered its municipal sovereignty to Los Angeles, on the promise that its canals would be restored and maintained. It was a promise unkept. Then oil was discovered. Amid the Venetian bridges and stonework, oil wells spurted up. The canals became not much more than open sewers.

The Grand Canal in its decline, ca. early 1930s.

The installation of oil wells along the Grand Canal, ca. 1930.

(Opposite)
Interior of a dance hall at Venice, ca. 1939.

Venice arcade, ca. 1939.

Aviation had been going strong in Los Angeles since the end of the war. The landscape was dotted with airports. The most notable in the 1920s were the fields maintained by director Cecil B. De Mille, an early flier, and Sid Chaplin, Charlie's brother, across from one another at the intersection of Wilshire Boulevard and Fairfax. When the developing city swallowed those sites, aviation had to move elsewhere.

Mines Field was a barley farm when, in 1927, it was designated by Los Angeles to be the official municipal airport. Nothing was there when sponsors of the 1928 National Air Races took over, but, by their completion, a field was in place. It was formally dedicated and opened in 1930.

No one was sure Los Angeles really had style, or if it was just posturing. In politics, no one was sure the city had postures, or if it was just styling.

In the late 1930s, German immigrants, especially German Jews, sought refuge from Hitler in Southern California. The government was indifferent to the plight of those prosecuted in their homeland. It seemed inconceivable that events in Germany would ever involve Los Angeles.

What impressed Los Angeles was a place like the Miracle Mile (Wilshire Boulevard between La Brea and Fairfax) so named because there were so many bargains, developers insisted, it was a miracle. Coulter's was the last word in 1938 Moderne architecture. Its front door typically opened on the parking lot at the rear.

Not everyone could shop with the fashionable. The Depression had hit the elderly the hardest and agitation among senior citizens for some form of relief had been persistent, at times desperate and unrealistic. Ham and Eggs promised the retired pay warrants once a week.

Much had been written about Los Angeles implying that the city was removed from, above and beyond, the rest of the nation. The Depression of the 1930s made it clear that Los Angeles was part of a larger economic community and what was true in economics here, applied in every other area as well. There was a style here, an essence, which stood out. But underneath it all, Los Angeles responded to the same forces of history, of economics, of society, that moved the rest of the society. As the area's most perspective commentator Carey McWilliams noted, "What America is, California is, with accents, in italics."

(Opposite)
The Los Angeles Plaza, Olvera Street, 1932. The city at the end of a harsh decade.

Central Avenue, heart of the city's black community, 1936.

(Above)
An adobe on New High Street in downtown, 1936.

The corner of Temple and Spring streets on the afternoon of August 15, 1936.

BE VIGILANT
NO LANDINGS ARE AUTHORIZED ON THIS BEACH
IMMEDIATELY
REPORT ANY BOAT ACTUALLY LANDING PERSONS ON SHORE HERE TO THE NEAREST MILITARY OR NAVAL POST AND TO THE SHERIFF AND POLICE FORCES
U. S. COAST GUARD
AUTO CLUB
SO. CAL.

IX

The War Years

In the nineteenth century, the far-sighted confidently predicted that the Pacific rim was destined to be the major stage of world history. Following the opening of the Panama Canal in 1914, Los Angeles eagerly anticipated an East-West trade which would one day dwarf that conducted out of the Eastern seaboard.

The Far East trade had not developed as expected. After a revolution in 1910, China had devolved into a hopelessly (in Western eyes) complex civil war. Japan, almost alone, became a steady customer.

The fulfillment of the Pacific's promised importance came with the outbreak of armed hostilities between Japan and China in 1931–32, in reality, the start of World War II. War fueled the engines of commerce and Los Angeles became an important observation post and transshipment point. Then, in 1941, the United States entered the war. History had at last smiled upon Los Angeles and placed it in the thick of the battle and the city relished the importance. As historian John Caughey has pointed out, war "was . . . the biggest thing that ever happened to Los Angeles."

Overnight the city was transformed from an urban center in which manufacturing lagged behind services to one sporting massive new heavy industrial installations, especially in aircraft and ships. Almost simultaneously, two armies moved in. One was a transient army of servicemen ever being shifted back and forth from the war zone, the other a civilian army of war workers, recruited from around the country, to man—and woman—the defense plants. The

Antisaboteur sign, ca. 1942. If the Japanese were coming, they'd land at Malibu and Venice and Manhattan Beach. With any luck they'd come on a summer weekend, and be lost in the crowds.

population of the city increased 400,000 between 1940 and 1950 and in the county of Los Angeles it nearly doubled. In just one industry, aviation, the number of employed increased from 20,000 before the war to 243,000 by the time the highest levels of production were reached.

The war on the home front was every bit as complex to wage as the battles staged overseas. Defense plants shifted to around-the-clock schedules necessitating a complex readjustment of the city's internal clock. The Pacific Electric streetcar system was called upon to provide transportation for huge numbers of people and, for the moment, the system's ridership levels returned to those of an earlier day, before the automobile's prominence. Yet, ironically perhaps, the first of the freeways, those great monuments to the car, was opened in 1940 and only the onset of war delayed their spread.

Psychologically the city was strained. Stress was difficult for city officials to manage. The political upheavals of the late 1930s which, by the start of the war, had forced major personnel changes in almost every area of city government complicated matters. Race relations were a particularly difficult area.

Despite the fact Los Angeles looked forward to trade with the Far East, the city, especially the city's best sort, looked down upon the trading partners. Los Angeles generally held the Chinese to be a contentious, disagreeable people who could learn only pidgin English and who should speak it only to missionaries. The Japanese were felt to be efficient but clannish and untrustworthy who spoke their English too precisely. The history of race relations can be summed up in a word: contempt.

With the outbreak of hostilities in the early 1930s, attitudes changed. The Chinese were increasingly a valiant, if still faceless, people. The 1930s were a boom time for Chinatown as Hollywood began churning out war movies and the demand for extras skyrocketed. The Japanese were villainous and treacherous and this was the best that was said of them. Race hatred in Los Angeles was an ascending curve before the outbreak of the war and immediately afterwards it became a near vertical line moving upwards. The apex was reached with the issuance by President Roosevelt of Executive Order 9066 which consigned Japanese-Americans to concentration camps.

As the war dragged on, racial enmity focused on Mexican-Americans who had long been targets of prejudice. If not easily enough singled out by their ethnicity, some Latino youths had taken to the wearing of the zoot suit, an exaggerated design which probably originated with poor whites in the South. In 1943, after a series of incidents involving servicemen on leave in the city and Mexican-Americans, which were made worse by sensational newspaper hysteria about an alleged "crime wave," rioting broke out. A week of street clashes marked the low point for the city in the war period. Of its contributions to winning the Pacific conflict, the city can be justly proud. But it was not a time free of all blemish.

When the war was won, Los Angeles realized that once again huge waves of immigration had remade the city. The new factories which had appeared were only the most visible sign of change. Beneath the surface, more profound alterations had been made in the character of the city.

Los Angeles' Pershing Square in downtown, ca. late 1930s. The rest of the world seemed far away and the city, even as it tooled up for war, was quiet.

In the war, Santa Monica would become famous as the home of Douglas Aircraft. The company had moved in the early 1920s to Wilshire Boulevard and Twenty-sixth Street, to what was then an empty field. In the late 1930s, Santa Monica was still just a peaceful beach suburb of Los Angeles. These were the last days when there was still an arm's length between the two cities.

Santa Monica harbor, in the late 1930s.

Santa Monica Boulevard in downtown Santa Monica, 1940.

Wilshire Boulevard in Santa Monica, Thursday afternoon, October 12, 1940.

The Arroyo Seco, a wash which ran between Pasadena and Los Angeles, was a quiet, charming locale. At one time, the municipalities which bordered the Arroyo Seco thought it would make a fine park. But the old river bed had another and ultimately more pressing use: it happened to be a convenient transportation route and in the late 1930s, planning for a parkway, later called a freeway, began. In December 1940, California governor Culbeth Olson came and took the first, and last, unimpeded trip along the new structure.

The motorcade which opened the completed structure, December, 1940.

(Opposite)
The Pasadena Freeway under construction.

Concrete was to become an ever-present fact of Los Angeles life. Concrete as poured and shaped into roads, highways, thoroughfares, and freeways. There was a slightly more pleasing, if slightly more fantastic use for the stuff. Theater owner Sid Grauman, impresses John Barrymore's profile into cement in the forecourt of Grauman's Chinese Theater in Hollywood, late 1940.

A display of military arms on the campus of UCLA, 1939. As the last good years ran out, the shadow of war appeared.

The Japanese had come to Los Angeles in the 1860s and, by the turn of the century, they were a small but significant part of the city's foreign-born population. A Little Tokyo district had formed downtown, around First and San Pedro streets. Japanese movies had been made in the small Japanese colony at the mouth of Santa Monica Canyon. In the 1920s and 1930s, a Japanese fishing community flourished at Fish Harbor on Terminal Island in the Port of Los Angeles. These were *nisei*, second-generation, Americans of Japanese ancestry.

(Opposite)
Mayor Fletcher Bowron receives a proclamation for Nisei Week, an annual celebration, 1940.

The main street of the Terminal Island Japanese community, ca. 1930.

(Above)
Fish Harbor, Terminal Island, the night of December 8, 1941, the night of the day war was declared.

Assistant Attorney General of the United States, Tom Clark, early February, 1942.

The accusations—more fantastic than the old familiar slurs—were that there were Japanese spies among the Americans down at Fish Harbor, watching the movements of the navy base; that a whole unit of Japanese infantry were secreted there in the garb of fishermen. Then came Executive Order 9066 and the investigations and, most absurd of all, the searching, the prying when it was obvious who the enemy was and he was thousands of miles away.

A raid by federal officials on a fisherman's home at Fish Harbor, December 1941.

Suspected enemy aliens rounded up by the Los Angeles Police, December, 1941.

(Opposite)
Evacuation of Japanese-Americans, 1942.

Boy Day on Terminal Island, ca. 1920s. Boy Day was one of the more colorful days in the Japanese community. Carp-shaped kites were flown on a day which celebrated the boys of each family. Carp-shaped kites flew and an American flag: tradition and loyalty.

Draftees outside Venice City Hall, November 11, 1941. Mobilization began.

Anna Mae Wong enlisting in Civil Defense, December, 1942. Civilians too were expected to enlist for the duration. For the Chinese community of Los Angeles, then about 5,000 strong, the gathering war clouds had early meant unexpected prosperity. In the 1930s, when war had broken out between the Chinese and the Japanese, Hollywood rushed to the front, or at least rushed in front of the cameras. For films such as *Oil for the Lamps of China*, extras were needed. Suddenly everyone in Chinatown was

in the movies. And none was more famous than Los Angeles' own Anna Mae Wong.

Mrs. Franklin D. Roosevelt addressing Civil Defense, December, 1941. Civil Defense was the special concern of the President's wife when she visited Los Angeles.

Jack Benny at Union Station, ca. 1942. Some contributed their blood, some their wisdom and others their wit and good spirits.

Los Angeles at war. Every man, woman and child was expected to do his or her part.

(Opposite)
Ship-building at San Pedro, ca. 1943.

(Above)
Interior of Pacific Electric terminal, ca. 1942.

Construction workers at San Pedro, ca. 1943.

Defense plant workers, 1941.

Not all the sights and sounds of wartime were of war.

(Opposite)
Soldiers on leave via the Pacific Electric, ca. 1943.

Victory Garden at 18th and Toberman streets in downtown Los Angeles, ca. 1943.

Dedication of Will Rogers State Beach, along the Pacific Coast Highway between Sunset Boulevard and Santa Monica Canyon, August, 1942. Will Rogers had been one of Los Angeles' own. It mattered not that he was born elsewhere; he belonged here.

(Above)
Department of Water and Power, Los Angeles, June, 1944. During a labor dispute in 1944, the army had to intervene and briefly take control of supplying Los Angeles with water and power.

The winners in the "Miss Carhop for 1942" contest at Santa Monica, September, 1942.

It was the afternoon of Thursday, April 12, 1945. The world looked brighter than it had in a long time. The war was close to over. That something had happened was announced by the screaming newsboys holding the special editions and the knots of people gathered to learn the few scraps of information available. The story was simple if sad: F.D.R. was dead.

Two views of a Los Angeles street corner, April 12, 1945.

Bob Hope entertains the troops one last time at the closing of the Hollywood Canteen, 1946.

The dedication of a defense plant, Long Beach, 1941.

X

The New Boom

"The modern city of Los Angeles," Charles Dwight Willard wrote in 1899, "may be said to have entered upon its career in 1888. Immediately prior to that time . . . lies the ancient Los Angeles, with material and social characteristics so radically different from those of the existing city that it is not possible to discover without some careful analysis how the present came to be generated out of the past." In taking 1888 as his starting point, Willard is referring to the conclusion of the boom of the 1880s, a wave of immigration which obliterated with ease and speed the Los Angeles which had existed just a few years prior, the "ancient Los Angeles."

Booms were, to the men of Willard's generation, common yet they struck a town only once, or at most, twice. Willard, founding secretary of the Chamber of Commerce, died before a very definitely extraordinary truth of the city's metabolism became clear: boom followed boom here, and after each, the Los Angeles of preboom times looked hopelessly ancient.

It was one thing to understand this and another for generations of Angelenos to experience it. When World War II ended, a new boom began and it was a boom which, within a few years, made clear it was the greatest of them all. And within those few years, a good part of Los Angeles was destroyed and the rest looked "ancient." Long-term residents, even natives, were surprised and looked around with amazement. Prewar Los Angeles was a matter of ancient history; wartime Los Angeles was rapidly disappearing and a new city was rising.

12727 Victory Boulevard in North Hollywood, San Fernando valley, 1947. Having commemorated victory in World War I, it now celebrated, in the endless new housing developments along its length, victory in World War II. In 1944, only 170,000 people lived on the other side of the Santa Monica mountains from Los Angeles in the San Fernando valley. By 1960, that figure was nearing one million.

War-workers and returning servicemen came here and stayed. In 1940, there were about 1,500,000 in the city of Los Angeles. By 1950, that had increased to 1,900,000 and, by 1960, the figure was 2,400,000. In the same period of time, however, the population of greater Los Angeles county jumped from 2,700,000 before the war to over 6,000,000 by 1960! Los Angeles was becoming a metropolis.

The earth shook and the sky roared and neither was in celebration of the end of the war. The tumult signaled the return of the Four Horsemen of Los Angeles: the Planner, the Developer, the Contractor and the Real Estate Agent. Vast fields decked in popular memory with wildflowers and grasses disappeared before their scythes. Farmers and their citrus groves were besieged and construction crews stood by impatiently as the last crop was harvested. Streets, sewers and sidewalks replaced plowed rows and irrigation ditches. In the 1880s, it was jokingly said that new subdivisions were laid out end to end all the way to the Mojave Desert. Now it was literally true and include Orange County to the south where it was increasingly hard to find an orange upon a tree.

To service the widely flung subdivisions, freeways were constructed, their prewar progenitor the Arroyo Seco Parkway renamed the Pasadena Freeway. Personal transportation, a euphemism for the hegemony of the automobile, was the order of the day, the concept which ruled the hearts and minds of planners, politicians and the public and the final death blow for fixed-rail transit.

Los Angeles filled in its blank spaces, the blank spaces in its geography and in its economy. Its business and social life was as complex and variegated as that of any other city in the world. Perhaps the last major American enterprise to come west was professional sports. First came the Cleveland Rams, then the Minneapolis Lakers and then the Brooklyn Dodgers, the very heart and soul of professional baseball. By the 1960s, the city had as complete a ledger of teams as any city in the United States and more than most.

Los Angeles more and more resembled the megalopolises of the East, one difference being the immutable sun. Los Angeles was trying its best to obliterate throwing up a cloud of chemicals, a blanket of airborne garbage called smog. Now the older residents remembered not only how beautiful was the city of ancient times, but also how clear.

New cities and new housing tracts as big as cities rose. One consisted of 3,000 acres and would accommodate 70,000 people. When construction crews set to work, a foundation was dug every fifteen minutes, 100 houses were begun in a day and, on one day in the late 1950s, 105 completed homes were sold. By 1960, this tract had blended into its nearest neighbors and, from ground level, was an indistinguishable part of the urban landscape.

Chavez Ravine in the late 1940s. A last look at ancient Los Angeles.

Housing under construction for later transportation to a site, Los Angeles, 1946.

Once the war ended, defense plants ceased around-the-clock operation and the crowds disappeared from the Pacific Electric streetcars. Moreover, the PE knew it had all but lost its competitive advantage over other methods of transportation: the unimpeded right of way. Cars had stolen that and streetcar–motorcar accidents had been a constant fact of life since the 1930s. Backing for the PE had been faint among bureaucrats and politicians and grew fainter as that great prewar dream of a network of freeways was revived. When the decision was made to deny streetcar routes down the median strips of new freeways, the PE was as good as dead. It would be charged the assassins were the Detroit car manufacturers and the Ohio tire companies. However much they might have helped, the deed was truly done by the Los Angeles public. Buses had actually began appearing in Los Angeles in the 1920s for even then it was evident fixed-rail transport could not be profitably expanded to everywhere people were living and working. Buses could go anywhere, even on the new freeways where they got in line along with the rest of the chronically stalled traffic.

The opening of a suburban bus route, ca. 1950s.

A PE bus of the 1920s.

The last streetcar through the Hollywood Subway, 1955. The Hollywood Subway was the closest Los Angeles ever got to a subway system. It stretched from the Subway Terminal Building on South Hill Street slightly more than a mile to the intersection of Beverly and Glendale boulevards. Built in 1925, it died in 1955. *Sic transis gloria mundis.*

Los Angeles had bought what social critic Louis Mumford has called "the absurd belief that space and rapid transportation are the chief ingredients of the good life." As greater Los Angeles formed from the process of building in all the open spaces which abutted neighborhoods and neighboring municipalities, the freeways were laid in to bind it all together. Throughout the 1950s and 1960s, the power of freeway planners was unquestioned. An irony was swept under the carpet: the freeways were obsolete, owing to the population growth, the minute the first draftsman set the first pencil to paper.

The Hollywood Freeway under construction, ca. 1951.

The Hollywood Freeway completed, ca. 1953.

(Opposite)
Looking east over downtown Los Angeles, ca. early 1960s.

A freeway interchange.

The end of the war had economists quaking and expecting the worst, at least recession, if not collapse. At first, labor unrest, the problems of reintegrating the work force, and declining employment seemed a confirmation of the gloomiest predictions. But before long, a successful conversion to peace by existing industries and the opening of major new plant, made clear Los Angeles was experiencing yet another boom.

(Above)
Strikers outside Columbia Studios in Hollywood, October, 1946. Strikes hit the motion picture industry at war's end.

"Liberal" Democratic California is a recent tradition. Historically the state had been a Republican stronghold.

Tumultuous postwar conditions offered the Democrats their best opportunity in years. But when the votes were counted, in 1946, a personable and ambitious State Attorney General, Earl Warren, had won election as governor. While Warren prided himself on his Republican "progressivism," the state nevertheless slid into a nightmare of political repression. A "Little Dies" committee, ignored during the war, succeeded in convincing the state legislature to adopt a loyalty oath. Investigations followed of a variety of alleged subversive activities, investigations spurred on by the House Un-American Activities' Committee's series of Hollywood witch hunts. By the late 1940s, it was clear that victims were demanded by politicians from the ranks of those whose politics the majority found

unacceptable or failed to understand.
The black list became a fact of life.
And in 1950, a young Congressman,
Richard Nixon, cynically manipulating
a crest of anti-Communism laced with
anti-Semitism, slandered his way into
the United States Senate.

(Opposite Left)
Two victims, Charlotta Bass, liberal,
editor of the state's major black-owned
newspaper, the *Eagle*, welcomes
singer, actor and political commentator
Paul Robeson to Los Angeles in 1949.

Of all the problems which confronted
postwar Los Angeles, the most
spectacular was the sudden
manifestation of smog. Well, not
exactly sudden for there'd been a day
during the war when a brown cloud
had settled unannounced upon the
city bringing tears and misery to all.
And even the Spanish, centuries
before, had noticed the odd manner in
which, on some days, the smoke from
Indian fires just hung in the air and
refused to dissipate.
By the early 1950s, smog was the
subject of furious city council debates
and endless newspaper features, crash
programs, governmental task forces,
and one new agency. As the years
passed, the debate grew increasingly
sophisticated and the smog worse.
Part of the problem was the way in
which the city disposed of its garbage:
by incinerating it. That realization

came early and by 1957, city council
succeeded in banning incinerators.
Then it was found the main cause of
smog was the automobile.

(Top Left)
An incinerator, ca. 1948.

Members of the city council
experiment with an innovative
approach to the problem, ca. 1954.

In 1938, a reform city administration in City Hall temporarily cracked the city's criminal syndicate open. A good number of the mobsters retired to Las Vegas. Crime in Los Angeles continued of course but for the moment less organized. After the war, it became obvious a new organization was forming, one with definite links to the older, well-organized crime syndicates of the East. Another similarity was the introduction of violence, especially of murder, to matters of local crime administration. In the old days, Los Angeles gangsters preferred to be shut of the glare gunplay tends to generate.
Four of the postwar era's most famous names when the subject was crime:

The body of Benjamin "Bugsy" Siegel at the Los Angeles County Coroner's, June, 1947. Siegel, active in bookmaking and Las Vegas casinos, had been glamorized in the 1930s after he'd been taken up by the social butterfly, the Countess di Frasso. In June of 1947, he was relaxing at the Beverly Hills home of his mistress, when persons unknown—but presumably associates—filled his person with buckshot. Some worried about the ominous nature of the crime; others fretted over its having been committed in sedate Beverly Hills.

Los Angeles Police Chief William H. Parker and his officers, ca. 1950. Parker was Los Angeles' most noted chief, of unquestioned integrity, and to him is given a large share of the credit for reinstilling professionalism and rebuilding morale in a badly shattered police force.

(Opposite)
Mobster Mickey Cohen at the funeral of one of his bodyguards, 1948. Cohen insisted he was just an honest haberdasher who ran a small shop on Sunset Boulevard. He would prove to be a mobster of singular staying power, having managed to escape half a dozen attempts on his life. In time, his moxie was rewarded and he was allowed to retire into the category of a colorful person.

Madame Brenda Allen (with bag over face) is escorted from her Hollywood brothel, ca. 1948. Allen, the town's most prominent madame had connections . . . everywhere. Her arrest triggered new charges of police and political corruption, in what weary newspapers called "The Vice Scandals of 1949."

First there was radio which was very popular for a long time. Cadillac dealer Don Lee purchased radio station KHJ in Los Angeles in 1927 and used it as the cornerstone in what became the West's first broadcasting network, the Don Lee System. In 1930, shortly after a curious invention called television had been demonstrated in New York, Lee set his engineers on the problem and, in mid-1931, they succeeded in transmitting the first televised images in the West. In December of 1931, Lee's W6XAO, experimental channel one, the first television station in Los Angeles, began broadcasting an hour a day, six days a week to the city's five television receivers.

Klaus Landsberg was an electrical genius in his native Germany. When the Nazis classified one of his innovations as a state secret, the enraged young Landsberg left the country. He encountered the fascinating new technology of television and, in 1941, was hired by Paramount Studios to organize and operate a new experimental station, W6XYZ. In 1943, W6XYZ went on the air. In time, Landsberg proved to be not only a technical innovator, but a crafty salesman of the new device as well. He realized its unique ability to feed remote news events into the home as demonstrated in 1947 when what was now being called KTLA reported live from the scene of a downtown explosion. It was

Landsberg who later organized the first telecast of an actual atomic bomb explosion.

A radio "man-on-the-street" broadcast, 1941.

An early Don Lee system remote telecast.

A "Televison Week" remote, Los Angeles, 1947, to promote the newest marvel of the age.

Klaus Landsberg, Alan Ladd and Veronica Lake on the set of "This Gun for Hire," the first such broadcast in history, 1943.

Reporter Dick Lane and an eyewitness at the explosion of an electro-plating plant on Pico Boulevard, 1947.

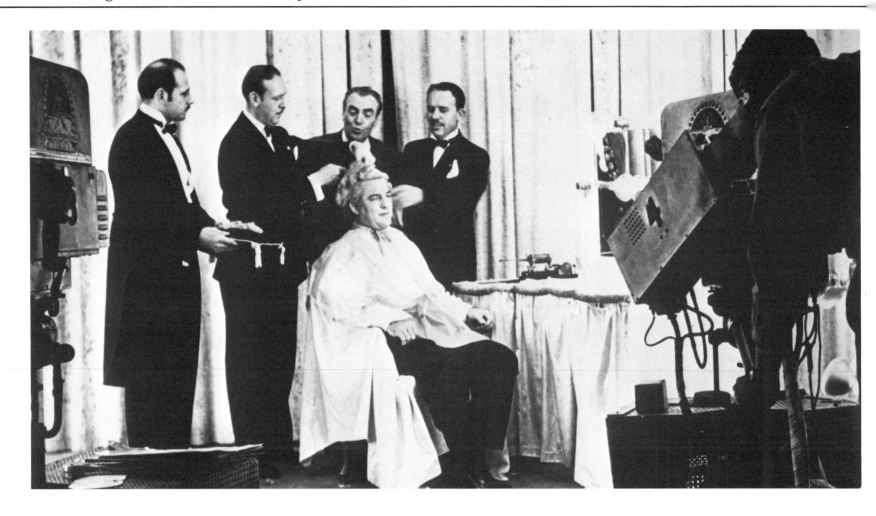

When the war ended, so ended the wartime freeze on the commercial propagation of television technology. In 1947, W6XYZ became the first Los Angeles commercial station and changed its call letters to KTLA (W6XAO ended up as KNXT). The honor of being the first sponsor of the first broadcast over the first station went, fittingly, to a car dealership, Tupman Motors. Tupman Motors no longer exists, but KTLA is still going strong.

Some of the stars of early Los Angeles television:

(Above)
Wrestling was the first sport which made its way to television and Gorgeous George one of the first television sports' stars. If his athletic ability left anything to be desired, his theatricality did not, and George realized and exploited his natural ability. Gorgeous George's locks are sheared for the camera, ca. 1950. Announcer Dick Lane, third from left, looks on.

"Hawthorne" on camera, ca. 1950. An original television anarchist, Hawthorne experimented with the

peculiarities of the medium to comic effect. His most notable pupil was Ernie Kovacs.

(Opposite Right)
Jack Bailey crowns a "Queen for a Day." Skillfully blending soap opera with reality, this program successfully crossed the waters separating radio from television, and became one of the young medium's longest-running hits.

(Top Left)
The crew of "Space Patrol," ca. 1952. One of the first serial hits on

television. At one time, the cast of "Space Patrol" was doing a local program, a radio program and a network program, all live.

Klaus Landsberg on left with Lawrence Welk, ca. 1950. Welk's "Champagne Music" was an early hit on KTLA and with it was born the modern variety show.

Spade Cooley opens a store in Hollywood, 1952. Cooley, a country-western singer, became KTLA's and Los Angeles' first television star. He

was awarded all the kudos which had been reserved only for the famous of the silver screen, chief of which in Los Angeles was promoting new businesses. The movie industry had only to look to see it was in deep trouble.

In 1908, the movies came to Los Angeles attracted by the prevailing, perpetual sun. In 1910, Hollywood annexed itself to Los Angeles at the same moment as film producer David Horsley moved his Nestor Film Company into an old tavern at the corner of Sunset and Gower. To Mr. Horsley falls the honor of operating the first film studio in Hollywood. In the next few years, the Vitagraph Company opened in Santa Monica, Universal in North Hollywood, Goldwyn in what became Culver City and a half-hundred other companies spotted themselves around Southern California. Together they became known as the film industry and the film industry, wherever located, forevermore bore the magic appellation of Hollywood. They were giants in those days: movies became one of Los Angeles' major industries. The studio owners were accorded the status that comes with wealth and some of the power too, but both grudgingly for proper Los Angeles always was slightly embarrassed by the bohemian enterprise that grew up in its midst. But for the world at large, Los Angeles was but a very small part of Hollywood. And it was Hollywood which, like the emerald city of Oz,

floated off the earth, beckoning, holding inside the jewel of fame and fortune.

(Opposite)
The Nestor Film Company, Sunset and Gower, Hollywood, ca. 1913.

From left to right: Will Hays, President Calvin Coolidge, Mrs. Coolidge, Mary Pickford and L.B. Mayer at MGM Studios, ca. 1925.

A banquet celebrating Paramount's Adolph Zukor's fiftieth year in motion pictures, 1937. From left, unidentified, Sam Goldwyn, George Jessel, Adolph Zukor, Darryl F. Zanuck, L.B. Mayer, unidentified.

(Above)
The Hollywood studios of Mary Pickford and Douglas Fairbanks showing the sets for Fairbanks' *The Thief of Bagdad*, ca. 1923.

Universal City in North Hollywood, ca. 1920.

Twentieth Century-Fox studios were built on the city's west side and, in those early days, had oil wells for neighbors and little else. Relentlessly, urbanization encapsulated the studio. Then, in the postwar era, television came along and the movie business nose-dived. Unfortunately, at the time, Fox was forty-eight million dollars in debt over its misbegotten spectacle *Cleopatra*. The studio backlot, executives realized, was a choice piece of real estate and too valuable for the troubled economics of movie-making. Fox sold. The wrecking ball was applied to the aging false fronts of the movie sets and from the tangled remain of dreams rose the business metropolis of the future, Century City.

Twentieth Century-Fox studios, ca. 1930s.

Fox management announces the development of Century City from the old Fox backlot, May 25, 1959.

The clearing of the Fox backlot: two views, ca. 1960.

(Opposite)
The cleared lot, ca. 1962. Santa Monica Boulevard to the left, to the right, Pico Boulevard.

Century City in the early 1970s. Behind and to the right, Twentieth Century-Fox. Was the reality greater than the dream?

In the land of promotions, the Tournament of Roses was, is, king. The idea had its birth in boredom. Pasadena's Valley Hunt Club found the mid-winter socially barren. A parade was decided upon, something for which the elite could dress in their finest. Since nothing was more locally boasted of than the flowers which grew in winter, roses were adopted as the motif. The first Tournament in 1890 was a grand success. Five years later, when the Club's interest in hosting the event faltered, the Pasadena Board of Trade, realizing the irresistible appeal to Eastern newspaper editors and their potential immigrant audiences, stepped in. A public subscription raised $595 and the parade's future was secured. In 1902 came an added dash of spice. College football was gaining wide popularity. The fearsome University of Michigan Wolverines were invited west and Stanford was offered up as opponent. More as sacrifice as matters turned out for Michigan won 49–0. The next year, Michigan was just as fearsome. Football was dropped but, in 1904, chariot racing was added, coincidentally about the time America became enthralled with the recently published *Ben Hur*. Between 1904 and 1915, Pasadena was the chariot racing capital of the world for what it was worth. While no one was killed in the annual saturnalia, the narrow escapes were many. But in the end, it was declining public interest that led to the reinstatement of football. In 1916, in a rainstorm, Washington State defeated Brown 14–0 and football was back to stay. And the parade? It remains its own fantastical self.

(Opposite)
The parade's first prize winner, 1890.

Hail to the victors, Michigan's 1902
football team.

The chariot race.

(Above)
Theme prize winner 1934. Theme:
Tales of the Seven Seas.

Long Beach entry, 1915.

Dinah Shore, 1956. Theme: Pages from
the Ages.

Up and down the West Coast, baseball meant the old Pacific Coast League. It was minor league ball in name only. It had a noble lineage, having been founded in 1903, and a long list of noble players including Steve Bilko, Billy Martin, Lefty O'Doul and Joe

DiMaggio. In a season that extended from March to November, P.C.L. teams played more than 225 games a year, compared to 150 of an average major league team today. The only reason the P.C.L. didn't become a separate, third major league was Eastern resistance to long travel times. Even so, in 1952, the P.C.L. was elevated from the status of a minor league and given "open" classification. It was about time. Los Angeles' two entries in the P.C.L. were a match for the majors. The fearsome Los Angeles Angels played at Wrigley Stadium near the Los Angeles Coliseum. The Hollywood Stars, a doughty congregation patronized by the entertainment industry, provided cross-town rivalry from their home at Gilmore Field, next to the Farmers Market.

Walter O'Malley, perhaps the shrewdest entrepreneur in the history of baseball, had a good idea. Ebbits Field in Brooklyn, home to his Dodgers, was an aging hulk and, despite loud protestations from the loyalists, support in Brooklyn for the Dodgers was on the decline. Los

Angeles looked inviting and especially inviting were the looks upon the faces of city officials at the mention of a plan which would get Los Angeles into the "big leagues." O'Malley convinced New York Giants owner Horace Stoneham to move to San Francisco. The die was cast and the fate of the P.C.L. sealed.

Chavez Ravine adjoined Elysian Park just north and east of downtown. The locals called it Palo Verde and it was a Mexican-American barrio that city fathers considered an eyesore. There were those who complained the city practically gave Chavez Ravine to the Dodger organization for a stadium and moved the residents out to complete the bargain.

Meanwhile, the Dodgers played at the Coliseum which, delightedly they realized, could hold more than 100,000. Perhaps not that many for baseball but enough so that when the Dodgers played the Giants in their first major league game in Los Angeles, an all-time attendance record was set. The Coliseum years were remembered for the absurd, 75-foot-high screen, the "Chinese Wall,"

which rose in the shortened left field,
the 1959 World Series in which the
Dodgers beat the White Sox before
immense crowds, and the pitching
brilliance of Sandy Koufax.
In 1962, Dodger Stadium in Chavez
Ravine opened. It was by common
consent, among the most beautiful
parks in baseball. And the team it
holds are now inseparably a part of
Los Angeles.

(Opposite)
Gilmore Field next to the Farmers
Market, 1957.

The final game at Gilmore Field, 1957.

The Chavez Ravine as it looked,
ca. 1946.

(Above)
Dodger Stadium, 1962.

The opening day of major league
baseball in Los Angeles, April 18,
1958, with San Francisco manager Joe
E. Lewis and Dodger manager
Walt Alston.

Los Angeles mayor Norris Poulson
throws out the first ball.

XI

Modern Mecca

Los Angeles' first set of parents, Latins both Spanish and Mexican, valued tradition over change. The Spanish laid out Los Angeles as mandated in the Laws of the Indies formulated in Madrid, which governed all aspects of a vast overseas empire. The town planning sections of this formidable code were promulgated in 1573 and were applied to every city the Spanish founded for over two hundred years. These regulations found their wisdom in traditional authorities from Machiavelli to the first century B.C. Roman architect Vitruvius. Tradition was all, and in accordance with tradition was Los Angeles created and so did she spend her first seventy-five years.

The Americans who wet-nursed the city's rebirth in 1850 had no compelling belief in tradition. Instead, they had an absolute faith in progress and in progress through commerce. America was rapidly becoming the most thoroughly commercial civilization in the world and, in the West, were its most doughty sons, feet firmly on the ground, faces resolutely pressed towards the future. They had little interest in the past and the Latin culture it held, for both lacked drive. Of course, a few touches were preserved for color especially for use in public relations.

So much has been said of Los Angeles' mastery of public relations and skill with advertising that it seems the city must have invented both. In fact, Los Angeles boosters represented a long tradition. The United States moved west from city to city as much as it did sod-buster to sod-buster and each new plat was the opportunity and the occasion for both a town promotion and, hopefully, a boom—however manufactured. Our pioneers were urban pioneers. Not those fleeing the mayhem of cities but those seeking to create that mayhem where nature seemed to have demanded it be: the American West, all the way to the Pacific Ocean. Town promotion had begun after the Revolutionary War, but really got going after the Civil War. Charles Dickens was suitably impressed with American town promotion madness to have included it as a piece in his *Martin Chuzzlewit*. By the time the boomers and boosters got to Southern California, all there was to know about town promotion had been learned.

Los Angeles advertised then, and in so doing, followed a hoary, perhaps the hoariest, of American traditions. There was nothing unique in this.

There are some other areas in which Los Angeles has received an overly exuberant reputation. Take the matter of growth. Los Angeles passed from pueblo to megalopolis in a hundred years. Phenomenal! Not really, for so have other cities and with growth rates equal to or greater than that experienced by Los Angeles. Nationally, urban growth has been the norm. Example: Los Angeles' average growth rate per decade between the turn of the century and 1930, as startling as it might appear, is matched by New York between the start of the 1800s and the end of that century.

Los Angeles is not quite as lily-white as it has been painted. It had a higher percentage of non-whites resident in 1930, for example, than did New York. Neither is Los Angeles the city of perpetual newcomers. The number of newcomers, depending on the era, is not out of line with other major cities. What this says is that Americans generally are a people on the move.

And what about those old jibes at provincial Los Angeles, the capital of Iowa, "double-Dubuque" as H.L. Mencken described the city? Sheer Mencken bunkum. In fact Los Angeles is one of the more cosmopolitan cities as it has consistently led the list of cities drawing the highest percentage of their population from other cities. We probably, relatively speaking, have more ex-New Yorkers in the 1980s than ever we did ex-Iowans in the 1920s. Perhaps they should consider forming borough clubs and holding picnics in Sycamore Grove as did the Iowans back in the 1920s.

What is the conclusion to be reached? That Los Angeles is not so very unique a place? No, rather that it is very much a part of tradition, a place with a history, a history of Spain and Mexico and the United States, a history which shapes its present and its future. As to being unique: Los Angeles exceeded the ability of the boosters and the boomers, even the professionals, to exaggerate. Here was a

place of unrivaled natural beauty. And while at first it seemed dry, without sources of energy and remote from trade lanes—an improbable site for a city—all that proved not to be true. There was plenty of water in subterranean deposits, astonishing amounts of oil, and a major harbor was easily constructed which became the natural focus of trade with the immense markets of Asia.

Los Angeles has color, character and style. It is a city with its own identity and it is that identity which has worked to help it solve many of the problems facing other cities. Where its institutions have faltered, the city's sense of its own worth has worked to pull it through. It is said by some that Los Angeles is the city of the future. Whether it is or not only time will tell but one thing can be said with certainty about that city of the future: it will think of itself much as Los Angeles does today.

(Above)
Food stand on Western Boulevard, Los Angeles, 1980.

(Opposite)
The Plaza in downtown Los Angeles, 1911.

The Plaza in downtown Los Angeles, 1980.

"[Los Angeles is] the product of one era of barbarism, two or three kinds of civilizations, and an interregnum." Benjamin F. Taylor, 1878.

"It was a grand play-country, and one could get along with less than in any other part of the United States and still be respectable and fat." Theodore S. Van Dyke, 1890.

"'Then what do you live on if you don't raise anything?' asked my friend.

'Credit. Haven't you been here long enough to learn that trick?'

'I exhausted mine sometime ago.'

'What are you doing then? . . .'

'Poising.

'Poising? What's that?'

'Did you ever see a hawk poising—hanging still in the air watching for something to drop on? That's my business at present.'" Theodore S. Van Dyke, 1890.

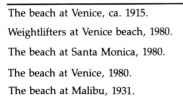

The beach at Venice, ca. 1915.

Weightlifters at Venice beach, 1980.

The beach at Santa Monica, 1980.

The beach at Venice, 1980.

The beach at Malibu, 1931.

"Health is lying around loose in Southern California." Anon. 1908.

"Census figures show that one out of every three people who have settled west of the Rocky Mountains during the past ten years has settled in Los Angeles County. The explanation of this unprecedented flow of population to one portion of the country is apparent: they are in search of human happiness." Los Angeles Chamber of Commerce, 1927.

Entrance to Twentieth Century-Fox Studios, 1980.

Street signs on the corner of Pico Boulevard and Motor Avenue, 1980.

Entrance to the Santa Monica Freeway in Santa Monica, 1980.

(Opposite)
The Super Yarn Mart, Gateway Boulevard and Barrington Avenue, West Los Angeles, 1980.

The first drive-in theater in California, on the corner of Pico and Westwood boulevards, 1934.

"The practice of making love on the highways is becoming alarmingly prevalent. In many cases it is flagrantly open." Captain Cannon of the Los Angeles motorcycle squad, Report to the Board of Supervisors, 1921.

"All your friends have motor cars, fleets of them, last year's and this year's models. The husbands use last year's models to run out to the studio and direct films or write scenarios or whatever they do. The wives use this year's ones to take you to Los Angeles in order to buy pins, or lunch or go to a matinee of a play just out from New York." Alice M. Williamson, *Alice in Hollywood*, New York: 1938.

"If California ever adopts a new state flower, the motor car is the logical blossom for the honor. . . . Whether commercially or socially, whether from the standpoint of business or sport, it is the same, the whole same and nothing but the same. All hail rubber! All hail the automobile!" Ernest McGaffey, "The Automobile Transforms Business," *Southern California Business* 11:7, August 1923.

Mannequins in a store window, Rodeo Drive, Beverly Hills, 1980.

Edgar Bergen and Charlie McCarthy at home, Beverly Hills, ca. 1930s.

Mural in East Los Angeles, 1980.

"I don't know whether I would like to know my neighbors here. I don't like the way some of them act." Ernest T. Emery, 1905.

"Los Angeles people do not carry arms. Indians are a curiosity, the gee string is not a common article of apparel here, and Los Angeles has three good hotels, twenty-seven churches, and 350 telephone subscribers." *Los Angeles Times*, 1883.

The construction of the Chandler Pavilion, Los Angeles Music Center, downtown Los Angeles, 1963.

The Chandler Pavilion of the Los Angeles Music Center, tenth anniversary, 1974.

"Here if anywhere else in America, I seem to hear the coming footsteps of the muses." William Butler Yeats, n.d.

"It is astonishing that people should devote themselves, as some do in Los Angeles, to the production of poetry, while there are many more profitable industries to be pursued. Corn, wheat, sugar beets, and many things else may be cultivated here with profit. Borax works and wool-scouring machinery ought to be introduced. There are sheep to be herded, grape vines to be trimmed, and many other things to be done that will yield a profit. Why then waste valuable time on poetry?" Editorial, *Los Angeles Express*, May 10, 1873.

The memorial service for Alfred Hitchcock, Beverly Hills, 1980.

Sign on Venice boardwalk, 1980.

The graves of Lankershim and Van Nuys, Evergreen Cemetery, 1980.

Evergreen Cemetery in East Los Angeles, 1980.

"Why *should* anybody die out here? They'll never get any closer to heaven." Edward Stewart White, *The Rose Dawn*, 1920.

Church in East Los Angeles, 1980.

Policemen on patrol in Venice, 1980.

Los Angeles City Hall and "Triforium," musical sculpture, downtown Los Angeles, 1980.

"Los Angeles is a city about which almost anything may be said either in praise or derogation; and about which a case can be made out either way." Charles Stoker, 1951.

"What America is, California is, with accents, in italics." Carey McWilliams, 1946.

Chronology

Don Antonio and Doña Mariana
Coronel, ca. 1886.

1769, August 1–3: Gaspar de Portolá and his band wandering in and about, make camp on what is now downtown Los Angeles.

1771, September 8: San Gabriel Mission is founded.

1781, September 4: The pueblo of Los Angeles is founded.

1822, December 8: The Church on the plaza in downtown Los Angeles is dedicated.

1836, January 21: Los Angeles is elevated from the status of a pueblo (town) to that of a ciudad (city).

1848: By treaty, California is ceded by Mexico to the United States.

1850: The first election of city officials under American laws is held.

1860, October 8: Los Angeles and San Francisco are linked by telegraph.

1869, October 26: Phineas Banning, developer of San Pedro as Los Angeles' harbor, inaugurates his Los Angeles and San Pedro Railroad, the area's first.

1869: The first franchise for a street railway, powered by horse, is granted by the city.

1871, October 24: A mob of angry white Angelenos lynches a score of Chinese.

1872: Los Angeles voters agree to subsidize the Southern Pacific in linking the city with the transcontinental railroad system via San Francisco. The vote is 1869 yea, 650 nay.

1876, September 5: The first train on the Southern Pacific leaves Los Angeles for San Francisco.

1882, April 15: The first Los Angeles telephone directory is issued.

1885, November 29: The first train of the Santa Fe enters Los Angeles.

1886: The first train loaded exclusively with oranges for eastern markets leaves Los Angeles via the Southern Pacific.

1892, November 4: Edward Doheny begins digging for oil within the city limits of Los Angeles.

1895: The Los Angeles and Pasadena Electric Railway, the first electric streetcar system, opens.

1899, April 26 and 27: Work begins at San Pedro on the construction of Los Angeles harbor.

1905, September 7: Voters in Los Angeles approve bonds for the construction of the Los Angeles Aqueduct.

1910, October 1: The *Los Angeles Times* is bombed in the midst of a bitter labor dispute and a score of workmen are killed.

1913, November 4: The Los Angeles Aqueduct is completed and water begins to flow.

1914, July 4: Director D.W. Griffith begins shooting his epic film *The Birth of a Nation* in North Hollywood.

1914: The first ship to journey to California via the newly opened Panama Canal docks at Los Angeles.

1920: Census figures show Los Angeles has finally outstripped San Francisco as the largest city in California.

1921, June 23: Royal Dutch Shell brings in the first well on Signal Hill in southern Los Angeles County. Over time, it will prove to be the most productive oil field ever found in the United States.

1923, New Year's Day: Sister Aimee Semple McPherson's Angelus Temple of the Four Square Gospel is dedicated.

1923: The first buses are seen on Los Angeles streets in an effort to extend the streetcar system.

1925: The Mulholland Highway along the crest of the Santa Monica mountains is formally opened.

1926: The cast of Eugene O'Neill's *Desire Under the Elms* is arrested and charged with presenting an obscene play.

(Above top)
The Lugo adobe in what was then Bell, California, ca. 1890.

(Above)
The Second Street cable car.

A casualty of Los Angeles' flood of 1914.

1927: The new, and still current, Los Angeles City Hall is dedicated.

1927: Ground breaking for the first building at the Westwood campus of the University of California at Los Angeles is held.

1930: Secretary of the Interior Ray Lyman Wilbur directs engineers to start construction on Boulder Dam, the first link in the Colorado River Project to bring water and electricity to Los Angeles.

1931: The city celebrates its 150th birthday.

1932: In mid-summer, the Games of the 10th Modern Olympiad are held.

1933: The first movie ever broadcast over television is shown on experimental station W6XAO-TV. It is *The Crooked Mile.*

1938: Mayor Frank Shaw is recalled from office and a reform administration under Fletcher Bowron is elected.

1939, May 3: Union Station passenger train terminal in downtown opens.

1940: The Arroyo Seco Parkway, later called the Pasadena Freeway, is opened.

Long Beach as it appeared in 1894.

1942: President Franklin D. Roosevelt signs Executive Order number 9066 ordering the internment of Japanese citizens.

1943: Race riots directed primarily at Mexican-American youths in Los Angeles break out.

1947, July 31: Charles Laughton opens in Bertolt Brecht's *Galileo* at the Coronet Theater on La Cienega Boulevard.

1951: "Golden Aerial Day" is celebrated in Los Angeles, the installation of a transcontinental microwave system which, among other things, will allow television sets in Los Angeles and New York to be tuned to the same program.

1957: The burning of garbage within city limits is outlawed.

1958, April 18: The Dodgers play their first major league game in Los Angeles.

1959: Redevelopment in the downtown Bunker Hill area is approved.

1963: The last Pacific Electric streetcar is retired from service.

1963: The Los Angeles Dodgers sweep the New York Yankees in the World Series 4–0.

1964: The Dorothy Chandler Pavilion of the Music Center is formally opened.

1965: Riots break out at 116th Street and Avalon in Watts.

1965, July 17: Simon Rodia, builder of Watts Towers, dies.

1970: Riots erupt in predominantly Chicano East Los Angeles.

1971: A major earthquake, centered in the Sylmar area, rocks Los Angeles.

1973, May 24: Thomas Bradley is elected mayor of the city.

1978: Los Angeles is selected to host the 1984 Summer Olympic Games.

1980, Sept.4: Los Angeles begins the celebration of its two hundredth anniversary.

The La Brea Tar Pits, 1922.

Bibliography

Los Angeles Coliseum, April 18, 1958. A record-setting opening day crowd of 78,672 witnesses a major league debut.

This book, being mainly pictorial, has only been able to suggest the general flow of Los Angeles history. And while it may be true that a good picture is worth 10,000 words, it's also true that the right 10,000 words are worth a great many pictures. The following is hardly a definitive bibliography but rather a few suggestions of works in which there are many good words.

Caughey, John and Caughey, LaRee. *Los Angeles: Biography of a City.* Berkeley and Los Angeles: University of California Press, 1977. A well-chosen collection of excerpts on various aspects of the city.

Cleland, Robert Glass and Dumke, Glenn S. *From Wilderness to Empire: A History of California.* New York: Alfred Knopf, 1959. An overview of the state.

Cleland Robert Glass. *The Cattle on a Thousand Hills: Southern California, 1850–1880.* San Marino, California: The Huntington Library, 1951. An excellent study of the first years of American rule.

Dumke, Glenn S. *The Boom of the Eighties in Southern California.* San Marino, California: The Huntington Library, 1944. Unfortunately out of print, it remains the most detailed study of the city's major real estate boom.

Fogelson, Robert M. *The Fragmented Metropolis: Los Angeles, 1850–1930.* Cambridge: Harvard University Press, 1967. Concentrates on political history.

Gebhard, David and Von Breton, Harriette. *L.A. in the Thirties 1931–1941.* Santa Barbara and Salt Lake City: Peregrine Smith, 1975. An architectural survey.

Grenier, Judson A., ed. *A Guide to Historic Places in Los Angeles County.* Los Angeles: Historical Society of Southern California, 1978. Valuable for the novice and the informed.

McWilliams, Carey. *Southern California: An Island on the Land.* Santa Barbara and Salt Lake City: Peregrine Smith, 1973. Still the best and most readable history, and commentary, on Los Angeles and Southern California.

Newmark, Harris. *Sixty Years in Southern California, 1853–1913.* Los Angeles: Zeitlin and Ver Brugge, 1976. A unique and greatly detailed memoir.

Nordhoff, Charles. *California for Health, Pleasure and Residence.* Tenspeed Press, 1973. A reprint of one of the great early books boosting Southern California.

Pitt, Leonard. *The Decline of the Californios.* Los Angeles and Berkeley: University of California Press, 1966. An excellent study of the end of the Spanish/Mexican culture.

Weaver, John D. *El Pueblo Grande: A Non-Fiction Book about Los Angeles.* Los Angeles: Ward Ritchie, 1973. A fast-paced overview of city history.

Some selected special topics:

Automobiles

Brilliant, Ashleigh. "Social Effects of the Automobile in Southern California during the 1920s." Ph.D. dissertation, University of California (Berkeley), 1964.

Booms and Boosters

Sunshine and Grief in Southern California, By An Old Promoter, Forty Years in the Field of Real Estate. Detroit: The St. Claire Publishing Co., 1931.

Baker, Charles C. "Rise and Fall of the City of Gladstone." Historical Society of Southern California, *Annual Publication* IX (1914).

Brook, Harry Ellington. *The City and County of Los Angeles.* Los Angeles: Los Angeles Chamber of Commerce. Various editions between 1890s and 1920s.

Van Dyke, T.S. *Millionaires of a Day: An Inside History of the Great Southern California Boom.* New York: Fords, Howard and Hulbert, 1890. A graceful and often extremely funny exposé.

Bunker Hill (Old Downtown Los Angeles)

Hylen, Arnold. *Bunker Hill, A Los Angeles Landmark.* Los Angeles: Dawson's Book Shop, 1976.

Crime and Punishment (sometimes)

Giesler, Jerry. *The Jerry Giesler Story.* New York: Simon and Schuster, 1960.

Robinson, W.W. *Lawyers of Los Angeles: A History of the Los Angeles Bar Association.* Los Angeles: Ward Ritchie Press, 1959.

Richardson, James H. *For the Life of Me: Memoirs of a City Editor.* New York: G.P. Putnam's Sons, 1954.

White, Leslie. *Me, Detective.* New York: Harcourt, Brace and Co., 1936.

Ethnic Groups

Dakin, Susanna Bryant. *A Scotch Paisano in Old Los Angeles: Hugo Reid's Life in California, 1832–1852, Derived from His Correspondence.* Berkeley and Los Angeles: University of California Press, 1978.

Heizer, Robert F. *Some Last Century Accounts of the Indians of Southern California.* Ramona, California: Ballena Press, 1976.

Mason, William. "The Chinese in Los Angeles." *Museum Alliance Quarterly* (Los Angeles) 6:2 (Fall, 1967).

———, and McKinstry, John A. *The Japanese of Los Angeles.* Los Angeles: Los Angeles County Museum of Natural History, 1969.

Vorspan, Max and Gartner, Lloyd P. *History of the Jews of Los Angeles.* San Marino, California: The Huntington Library, 1970.

Photography

Hill, Laurance, ed. *La Reina: Los Angeles in Three Centuries.* Los Angeles: Security First National Bank, 1929.

Robinson, W.W. *Panorama: A Picture History of Southern California.* Los Angeles: Title Insurance and Trust Co., 1953.

Watson, Delmar, ed. *"Quick Watson, The Camera."* Hollywood: Delmar Watson, 1975.

Trains and Trolleys

Bradley, Bill. *The Last of the Great Stations.* Los Angeles: Interurbans Publications, 1979.

Crump, Spencer. *Ride the Big Red Cars: How Trolleys Helped Build Southern California.* Los Angeles: Crest Publications, 1962.

Myers, William A. and Swett, Ira L. *Trolleys to the Surf: The Story of the Los Angeles Pacific Railway.* Los Angeles: Interurbans Publications, 1976.

Seims, Charles. *Mount Lowe: The Railway in the Clouds.* San Marino, California: Golden West, 1976.

Water

Nadeau, Remi A. *The Water Seekers.* Santa Barbara and Salt Lake City; Peregrine Smith, 1974.

Kahr, William L. "The Politics of California Water: Owens Valley and the Los Angeles Aqueduct, 1900–1927." *California History* (Spring and Summer, 1976).